Gambling
102

Gambling 102

The Best Strategies for All Casino Games

Michael "The Wizard of Odds" Shackleford

Huntington Press
Las Vegas, Nevada

Gambling 102
The Best Strategies for All Casino Games

Published by
   Huntington Press
   3687 S. Procyon Ave.
   Las Vegas, NV 89103
   Phone (702) 252-0655
   e-mail: books@huntingtonpress.com

ISBN: 0-929712-07-2

Cover Photo supplied by Stockbyte™ Royalty Free Photos

Cover Design: Bethany Coffey & Laurie Shaw
Interior Design & Production: Laurie Shaw

Acknowledgements

Special thanks to: The Los Alamitos High School math department, whose example and inspiration almost led me to be a high school math teacher myself.

The Society of Actuaries for 11 challenging actuarial examinations, without which I probably would have forgotten most of my math skills.

The gambling experts who came before me and showed me by example how to use math to study games of chance, in particular Stanford Wong and Peter Griffin.

My Web site readers for providing information and encouragement, and for correcting my occasional mistakes.

Don Schlesinger for always keeping me on my toes when it comes to blackjack. Blair Rodman for his help with poker. Fezzik and Joel Brewster for their help with sports betting. Michael Bluejay, Anthony Curtis, and Deke Castleman for their editing. Anthony Curtis for taking a chance on publishing a book by a name largely unknown outside of the Internet.

My parents, who are nervous about betting $5 on the Super Bowl, but have in general supported whatever I do.

And finally my wife Onalisa, for reluctantly letting me uproot the entire family to pursue my ambition as a gambling writer and consultant.

Contents

Introduction

This book is the product of years of mathematical analysis, computer modeling, and actual casino play. In 1997 I began analyzing several popular casino games as a mental challenge. Having just completed the actuarial examinations, I was eager to put my mind to use on other practical math applications. After arriving at what I felt was the best strategy for several games, I searched the Internet for a source to compare my work against. My search led to absolutely nothing of value. All I found were charlatans pitching worthless systems to alledgedly beat the casinos. I felt that I could easily provide information better than anything on the Internet at that time, so I did.

My Web site began on my personal two-megabyte account through my Internet access provider, Charm Net out of Baltimore. With no advertising effort I got lots of traffic and built a loyal following. My visitors challenged me to add new games and analyze unusual rules variations, and sometimes identified mistakes in my own math. Later I moved to my own domain name, thewizardofodds.com, and to the chagrin of some, began accepting advertisements. In the March 2001 issue of *Casino Player* magazine, my Web site was voted the "Best Gambling Strategy Site." In 2003, my Web site moved again, this time to wizardofodds.com (no more "the").

This book assumes that the reader already knows the

rules of the games. Plenty of books on the market explain the rules—that's Gambling 101. *Gambling 102* takes you to the next stage—the point at which you're playing the games in the best possible manner for the least amount of effort. Every game has a best possible way to play. Sometimes—as is the case with blackjack card counting, for example—the best strategy will require that you study even further. But for most games, the best strategy is easy to implement and even easier to access, because it's right here within these pages.

The information in this book is the result of not only my own work, but that of thousands of other math-minded gamblers who have commented on and helped me improve my original work. If you believe in predetermination, following hunches, or that there's an easy way to beat the casinos, then you probably need another book. But if you believe that mathematics provides the best way to approach games of chance, then this is the book for you. Let my years of effort improve your gambling knowledge, and don't be surprised when you notice a dramatic improvement in your results.

A Word About the Bell Curve

The three most important factors affecting how much a player wins or loses when gambling are as follows:

1. The choice of game.
2. The player's skill in that game.
3. Random mathematical variance (what a layman calls "luck").

In the short run, factor 3 has the greatest influence. In the long run, factors 1 and 2 play the pivotal role. Successful gamblers have a long-term perspective. They don't overbet their bankrolls, so they're able to ride out the short-term ups and downs. The more they play, the deeper into the long run they get and the closer their average results approach the mathematical expectation. While I can't help you with factor 3, I *can* help with factors 1 and 2. Showing players how to choose a low house-edge game and play it well is what this book is all about.

The outcome of a series of bets is like a point chosen at random on a bell curve—a concept known in statistics as the Central Limit Theorem. The expected return of every game and every strategy has its own bell curve. The lower the house edge, the greater the mean (average result) of the curve is. The greater the variance (risk), the more spread out the bell curve is. As a player, your goal should be to get on the bell curve with the highest mean possible. In non-mathematics talk: If you play in the best situations, the more you play, the better your results will be.

1

The Ten Commandments of Gambling

While climbing Mount Charleston, I came across a burning slot machine. A voice emanated from the fire, identifying itself as the God of Averages. This is what I was told to say in this book.

    I   Thou shalt honor thy gambling debts.
    II   Thou shalt expect to lose.
    III Thou shalt trust the odds, not hunches.
    IV Thou shalt not overbet thy bankroll.
    V   Thou shalt not believe in betting systems.
    VI Thou shalt not hedge thy bets.
    VII Thou shalt covet good rules.
   VIII Thou shalt not make side bets.
    IX Thou shalt have good gambling etiquette.
    X   Thou shalt tip.

Having fulfilled my obligation to the God of Averages, here are my further comments on each commandment.

I *Thou shalt honor thy gambling debts.*

A true gentleman honors his debts, especially gambling debts. When making a bet with another person, you're putting your honor on the line to pay if you lose. No excuses!

II *Thou shalt expect to lose.*

The Las Vegas Strip was not built by winners. Even with good rules and strategy, the odds are still usually in the casino's favor. So don't get mad if you lose. Think of it as the price you pay for entertainment.

III *Thou shalt trust the odds, not hunches.*

If you want to maximize your odds, then believe in mathematically proven strategies, not hunches. If hunches work, why are so many psychics still working the Boardwalk in Atlantic City rather than playing in the casinos and making a profit?

IV *Thou shalt not overbet thy bankroll.*

Before playing, determine what you can safely afford to gamble with as entertainment money. Stick to your limits and don't gamble with money you need for necessities.

V *Thou shalt not believe in betting systems.*

For every one legitimate gambling writer there are a hundred charlatans trying to sell worthless betting systems that promise an easy way to beat the casinos. I know it's a cliche, but if it sounds too good to be true, it probably is.

VI *Thou shalt not hedge thy bets.*

Hedge bets invariable carry a high house edge. For example, never take insurance in blackjack and never bet the any craps or any seven in craps.

VII *Thou shalt covet good rules.*

Rules vary from casino to casino. To improve your odds (and results), know good rules from bad, then seek out and play the best rules possible.

VIII *Thou shalt not make side bets.*
Side bets are sucker bets. Period.

IX *Thou shalt have good gambling etiquette.*
Gambling is a lot more fun when people are polite and respect each other. For more on this, see the appendix on gambling etiquette (Appendix G).

X *Thou shalt tip.*
Dealers generally make only minimum wage and count on tips to earn a decent living. Although the amount to tip is subject to much debate, the reason for tipping should be based on good service, not how much you win or lose. Not to tip is to steal the dealer's service.

2

Baccarat

Baccarat is easy to play and has a low house edge. However, if you want a game of skill, baccarat may quickly become as boring as betting on the toss of a coin.

Traditional (sometimes called "big") baccarat is usually played in snooty roped-off areas of casinos and has high minimum bets, often between $100 and $1,000. For players of more modest bankrolls, there's "mini-baccarat," which can usually be found on the main casino floor among the other table games. The rules are the same no matter which you play; however, there are some procedural differences. For example, in regular baccarat the players deal the cards themselves, while in mini-baccarat the dealer handles everything. Either way, baccarat is a game based entirely on luck.

Both big and mini-baccarat have only three bets: banker (or bank), player, and tie. Table 1 shows payoffs for each bet, the probability of winning, and the house edge, based on a game dealt with 6 decks.

TABLE 1—Baccarat Probability and Edge

Bet	Pays	Probability of Win/Loss/Tie	House Edge
Banker	19 to 20*	45.87%/44.63%/9.51%	1.06%
Player	1 to 1	44.63%/45.87%/9.51%	1.24%
Tie	8 to 1	9.51%/90.49%/0.00%	14.44%
*or even-money less a 5% commission			

Baccarat hands are played out by a mandatory set of rules that are the same wherever you play it. The edge can vary slightly depending on how many decks are used. Eight decks are most commonly used in big baccarat, while 6 decks are the norm in mini-baccarat. Some Internet casinos use only 1 deck. Table 2 shows the house edge on all three bets according to the number of decks.

TABLE 2—Baccarat Edge by Number of Decks

Decks	House Edge Banker	Player	Tie*
1	1.01%	1.29%	15.75%
6	1.06%	1.24%	14.44%
8	1.06%	1.24%	14.36%

*Tie pays 8-1.

For several years, Binion's Horseshoe in downtown Las Vegas charged only a 4% commission, resulting in a house edge of .60% on banker bets. Other casinos have experimented with 3% commissions. In 1989, the Las Vegas Sahara offered commission-free banker bets up to $100, which yielded a player edge of 1.24%. That was an excellent deal for players, which predictably did not last long. Table 3 shows the house edge on the banker bet, based on 6 decks, according to various commission charges.

TABLE 3—Baccarat Edge by Commission

Commission on Banker	House Edge
0%	-1.24%
1%	-0.78%
2%	-0.32%
3%	0.14%
4%	0.60%
5%	1.06%

A negative house edge indicates a player advantage.

The pay on a tie bet can also vary. Some casinos used to offer 9-1 on ties, until they found that the bet at that payoff was vulnerable to card counting. (With current standard pay-tables, counting cards at baccarat is useless for identifying an edge on any bet.) Table 4 shows the house edge on the tie bet, based on 6 decks, according to various payoffs.

TABLE 4—Edge on Tie

Tie Pays	House Edge
7-1	23.95%
8-1	14.44%
9-1	4.93%
10-1	-4.58%

No-Commission Baccarat

In an attempt to eliminate the pesky 5% commission on the banker bet, various versions of commission-free baccarat have been introduced.

The first variant, offered in Singapore, pays 1-2 when the banker wins with 8. This results in a house edge of 4.07%. I saw a similar rule at the Atlantic City Hilton where a banker win paid 1-2 on a 6, for a house edge of 1.46%. I've heard they pay 1-2 on a 5 in the Netherlands, for a house edge of .93% (which, surprisingly, is better than regular baccarat.

In the second variant, both the banker and player follow conventional player rules, except that a winning 3 on either hand results in a push. The house edge on both banker and player bets in this case is 1.54%.

The third variant showed up at the Las Vegas Plaza in 2004. Banker rules are conventional, except a winning 7 com-posed of three cards is a push instead of a win. This results in a house edge of 1.02%, slightly better than standard bac-carat. This game also offers a side bet on a three-card winning banker total of 7 that pays 40-1, for a house edge of 7.61%.

Lucky Pair

Some casinos offer a baccarat side bet that a player or bank's first two cards will be a pair. Most side bets in table games carry a hefty house edge, and the Lucky Pair bet is no exception, as Table 5 shows.

TABLE 5—Lucky Pair Probability and Edge

Bet	Probability of winning	Pays	House Edge
Banker pair	7.47%	11 to 1	10.36%
Player pair	7.47%	11 to 1	10.36%
Either pair	14.38%	5 to 1	13.71%

Strategy

Optimal strategy in baccarat is simple: Bet on the banker hand every time. You'll see other players religiously taking notes and tracking every hand dealt from the shoe, but their

TABLE 6—Baccarat Edge for Blended Bets

Ratio of bets on bank	Ratio of bets on player	Average house edge
0%	100%	1.24%
10%	90%	1.22%
20%	80%	1.20%
30%	70%	1.19%
40%	60%	1.17%
50%	50%	1.15%
60%	40%	1.13%
70%	30%	1.11%
80%	20%	1.10%
90%	10%	1.08%
100%	0%	1.06%

search for trends is a waste of time. If you want to make occasional bets on the player, it won't cost very much in expected value. Table 6 shows the expected value for bouncing back and forth between the bank and player bets according to the ratio of bank to player bets that you make. You should definitely avoid the tie bet at all costs.

Summary

The best strategy in baccarat is to bet on the banker every time. And don't be fooled by the no-commission games; the regular game is a better bet.

3

Big Six

Big six, sometimes called the wheel of fortune, looks like a big carnival-game wheel. Of the 54 stops on the wheel, 52 have inlaid paper money in denominations from $1 to $20. The other two stops are a joker and a "logo." All players have to do is bet on which denomination or symbol the wheel will stop on. What you bet on is exactly what you win per $1 wagered if the wheel stops there. Table 7 shows the betting options, their payoffs, the probability of winning, and the house edge. The 40-1 payoff for the joker and logo are common in Las Vegas. In Atlantic City and some other places (e.g., Harrah's in New Orleans), the joker and logo pay 45-1, lowering the house edge on that bet to 14.81%.

TABLE 7—Big Six Probability and Edge

Bet	Pays	Probability	House Edge
$1	1-1	44.44%	11.11%
$2	2-1	27.78%	16.67%
$5	5-1	12.96%	22.22%
$10	10-1	7.41%	18.52%
$20	20-1	3.70%	22.22%
Joker/Logo	40-1	1.85%	24.07%
Joker/Logo	45-1	1.85%	14.81%

Strategy

The only realistic strategy for the big six is to stick to the bet with the lowest casino edge: the $1 spot.

If a dealer could be found with a consistent force-per-spin, it would be possible to gain an advantage. The only bets vulnerable to this kind of prediction are the joker and the logo, especially when the more generous Atlantic City payoffs are in force. "Wheel watchers" attempt to estimate where the wheel will stop based on the wheel's present position and the average revolutions per spin. Since the joker and logo are located on opposite sides of the wheel, the strategy should be to bet on either the joker or logo, whichever is closer to the estimated stopping point. It's common procedure for dealers to alternate spinning clockwise and counterclockwise, so it's necessary to be alert to how direction relates to the predicted number of revolutions.

Table 8 shows the player's expected return for betting on joker or logo under Las Vegas and Atlantic City rules according to the accuracy of this type of prediction. "Accuracy" refers to the percentage of time that the spot wagered on lands in the top half of the wheel. Without having any special ability to predict the outcome, you will have 50% accuracy just from random spins. As you can see from the chart, you must

TABLE 8—Big Six Prediction Accuracy/Edge

Accuracy	Las Vegas	Atlantic City
50%	-24.07%	-14.81%
55%	-16.48%	-6.30%
60%	-8.89%	2.22%
65%	-1.30%	10.74%
70%	6.30%	19.26%
75%	13.89%	27.78%
80%	21.48%	36.30%

be able to predict at slightly better than a 65% rate to have an advantage with Las Vegas payoffs, and at about 60% to have an advantage with Atlantic City payoffs. Hence, this is not a strategy that most will be able to implement with success.

Summary

Overall, big six offers the worst odds among all the table games. However, if you must play, the best bet is on the $1. If you find a dealer who spins with revolutions that are consistent to within half a spin, bet on joker or logo, whichever you determine a consistent spin will cause the wheel to land closer to.

4

Blackjack

Blackjack is the most popular casino table game in the
United States and with a little effort, players can enjoy a
low house edge of .2% to .7% — depending on the rules of the
blackjack game being played. Once the basics are mastered,
diligent players can gain an advantage by learning a card-
counting strategy.

Blackjack rules often vary from city to city, casino to casino, and table to table. While most players will plop down
and play at any table, the discriminating gambler should be
willing to walk a few extra steps to find the game with the
best rules. How great can the disparity be from one game to
another? The difference between the best and worst games
that I know at the time of this writing follow:

Rule	Barona	Rio
Decks	1	1
Blackjack pays	3-2	1-1
Dealer soft 17	Hits	Hits
Double any first two cards	Yes	Yes
Double after split	Yes	No
Late surrender allowed	Yes	No
House Edge	.02%	2.5%

The Barona casino is in San Diego county and the Rio is in

Las Vegas. Not all tables at Barona and Rio follow the same rules, these are just the extremes. In fairness to the Rio, the blackjack game listed is in its bikini pit, which should result in some added entertainment value.

In recent years, blackjack rules (as well as the rules for other games) are becoming stingier. In particular, most casinos now hit soft 17, a rule that strongly favors the casino. The rule has become so prevalent that I now include it in the benchmark rules for the standard blackjack game. Unless otherwise stated, all discussion in this chapter will be based on the following "Las Vegas Benchmark Rules."

1. 6 decks
2. Dealer hits soft 17
3. Player may double on any first two cards
4. Player may double after split
5. Player may split up to three times (to make four separate hands)
6. Aces may be split only once and only one card is drawn to each split ace
7. Surrender allowed

Shuffling

There are three ways any card game can be shuffled:

1. A hand shuffle—This is the traditional shuffle performed by a dealer.
2. An "automatic" shuffle—This shuffle is done by a machine that shuffles 1 to 8 decks at once. A table using an automatic shuffler usually rotates two shoes of different colored cards—while one is being played the other is being shuffled. Mathematically, it's the equivalent of a hand shuffle.

3. A "continuous" shuffle—This shuffle is performed by
a machine that randomly inserts discards back into the
shoe. Most machines use five decks, but some use two
to four decks. Mathematically, it's the equivalent of
shuffling after every hand.

As we will see, the shuffling method may have an influence on the house edge.

The House Edge

The basic strategy presented later in this chapter shows
how to play every possible hand against any dealer up-card.
Using this strategy with the Las Vegas benchmark rules, the
house edge is about one-half of one percent. A less-compli-
cated "simple strategy" will also be presented later. Table 9
shows the house edge for the basic strategy, the simple strategy, and some ill-advised alternative strategies.

TABLE 9—Blackjack Edge vs. Different Strategies

Strategy	House Edge
Basic strategy	0.53%
Simple strategy	1.03%
Never double or split	2.42%
Never bust	4.00%
Mimic the dealer	5.67%

The late Peter Griffin, one of the greatest minds in blackjack, did a study based on the observation of 11,000 hands
of actual play, which appears in his book, *Extra Stuff*. Griffin
concluded that strategy mistakes result in the average player
losing an extra 1.4% beyond the house edge for basic strategy.
Hence, the saving the recreational player can realize by learning the basic strategy is worth the effort many times over.

Rules Variations

Blackjack rules vary widely from casino to casino, and even from table to table. The most significant variations are in the number of decks being dealt (the fewer the better for the player), dealer hits or stands on soft 17 (standing favors the player), and whether or not doubling after splitting is allowed (doubling favors the player). Table 10 shows the most

TABLE 10—Effect of Rules on Blackjack Edge

Rule	Effect
1 deck	+0.51%
2 decks	+0.20%
4 decks	+0.05%
Continuous shuffler*	+0.03%
5 decks	+0.02%
8 decks	-0.02%
Dealer stands on soft 17	+0.22%
Player may draw to split aces	+0.19%
Player may resplit aces	+0.08%
Player may not surrender	-0.09%
Player may split only 2 times	-0.01%
Player may split only once	-0.05%
Player may double on 9-11 only	-0.10%
Player may not double after splitting	-0.14%
Player may double on 10,11 only	-0.19%
Blackjack pays 6-5**	-1.39%
Blackjack pays even money**	-2.32%

* *Based on 5-deck game*
* * *Based on single-deck game*

common variations and their effect on the player's expected return relative to the Las Vegas benchmark (except where noted). A positive effect in the chart is good for the player. Multiple rules changes may result in an interaction effect, making the total change more or less than the sum of the individual changes, but deriving a cumulative total provides a good estimate.

Look for games where the dealer uses 2 decks or less or stands on soft 17. Or better yet both. And above all, avoid the dreaded single-deck games that pay only 6-5 on blackjacks.

The 6-5 Payoff

These days, many casinos display prominent signs that read "Single Deck Blackjack." However, much smaller signs read "Blackjack Pays 6-5." On a single-deck game paying the traditional 3-2 for naturals, the house edge is 0.19%. However, the 6-5 payout on blackjacks costs the player an additional 1.39%, for a total house edge of 1.58%. At some of these games, a player blackjack always wins, which lowers the house edge by 0.21% to 1.23%. Either way, 6-5 is a horrible rule that doubles or triples the house advantage. I urge you to go nowhere near this game.

Strategy

Blackjack strategy can vary from extremely simplistic — e.g., simply mimicking the way the dealer plays — to powerful counting techniques, such as the Hi-Opt II system. Here I present two strong intermediate strategies: the simple strategy and the basic strategy.

The Simple Strategy

The following simplified strategy correctly indicates how

to play most hands in blackjack. The house edge with this strategy is 0.93% against the Benchmark Las Vegas Strip rules.

1. Stand on hard 12-16 against dealer 2-6.
2. Double on 10,11 against dealer 2-9.
3. Always split 8s, 9s, and aces.
4. Stand on soft 18 or more.
5. Stand on hard 17 or more.
If rules 1-5 do not apply, hit.
Never take insurance.

The Basic Strategy

The basic strategy is the foundation of all good blackjack play. It was first published in the *Journal of the American Statistical Association* in September 1956. Since then, it's appeared in numerous gambling books and been memorized by untold numbers of players.

To use the basic strategy, look up your hand along the left-most column and the dealer's up-card along the top. In both cases, an "A" stands for ace. From top to bottom are the hard totals, soft totals, and hands that can be split. Soft hands include an ace and can't be busted by drawing a single additional card (A,7 and A,3,4 are soft hands; A,7,5 is not). The basic strategy in Table 11 is designed for the benchmark Las Vegas Strip rules. Rule variations can change the proper play in some borderline situations, but these strategy exceptions make only a marginal difference in the house advantage. See Appendix A for basic strategy tables for alternative numbers of decks and games in which the dealer stands on soft 17.

Some hands where the proper play is obvious have been left off the table to save space. In particular, always hit hard 8 or less, always stand on hard 18 or more, and always stand on soft 19 or more.

TABLE 11—Basic Strategy 6-Deck Benchmark

Your card	2	3	4	5	6	7	8	9	10	A
				Dealer's hand						
9	H	D	D	D	D	H	H	H	H	H
10	D	D	D	D	D	D	D	D	H	H
11	D	D	D	D	D	D	D	D	D	D
12	H	H	S	S	S	H	H	H	H	H
13	S	S	S	S	S	H	H	H	H	H
14	S	S	S	S	S	H	H	H	H	H
15	S	S	S	S	S	H	H	H	R/H	R/H
16	S	S	S	S	S	H	H	R/H	R/H	R/H
17	S	S	S	S	S	S	S	S	S	R/S
A,2	H	H	H	D	D	H	H	H	H	H
A,3	H	H	H	D	D	H	H	H	H	H
A,4	H	H	D	D	D	H	H	H	H	H
A,5	H	H	D	D	D	H	H	H	H	H
A,6	H	D	D	D	D	H	H	H	H	H
A,7	D/S	D/S	D/S	D/S	D/S	S	S	H	H	H
A,8	S	S	S	S	D/S	S	S	S	S	S
2,2	P	P	P	P	P	P	H	H	H	H
3,3	P	P	P	P	P	P	H	H	H	H
4,4	H	H	H	P	P	H	H	H	H	H
5,5	D	D	D	D	D	D	D	D	H	H
6,6	P	P	P	P	P	H	H	H	H	H
7,7	P	P	P	P	P	P	H	H	H	H
8,8	P	P	P	P	P	P	P	P	P	R/P
9,9	P	P	P	P	P	S	P	P	S	S
10,10	S	S	S	S	S	S	S	S	S	S
A,A	P	P	P	P	P	P	P	P	P	P

Never take insurance

Key to table:

- H   Hit
- S   Stand
- D   Double if allowed, otherwise hit
- D/S Double if allowed, otherwise stand
- P   Split
- R/H Surrender if allowed, otherwise hit
- R/S Surrender if allowed, otherwise stand
- R/P Surrender if allowed, otherwise split

Shufflers

Although hated by many players, continuous shufflers actually reduce the house edge. The reason for this is that slightly more large cards come into play on average in a continuously shuffled game (due to fixed shuffle points on normally shuffled shoes), and large cards favor the player. In a 5-deck game, a shuffler reduces the house edge by 0.03%. In many casinos, the options are playing an automatic or hand-shuffled 6-deck game or a 5-deck game with a continuous shuffler. In this situation one less deck is worth 0.02% and the shuffler is worth 0.03%, so the total house edge on the continuous-shuffler game is 0.05% less. However, a game with either type of machine shuffler probably has more hands dealt per hour, resulting in greater total expected losses given the same amount of playing time. Obviously, trying to count cards in a continuously shuffled game is hopeless.

Side Bets

Let me make one thing perfectly clear: Never make a side bet in blackjack (or any game for that matter). The only exceptions are progressive-based side bets when the meter reaches unusually high amounts, which happens so rarely it's not worth discussion. Side bets (including insurance) traditionally carry big edges for the house. Table 12 shows the house edge on some of the common blackjack side bets that you will encounter. Paytables may vary; Table 12 is based on common rules at the time of this writing (see wizardofodds.com for the paytables used).

Card Counting

Serious players cannot gain an advantage by counting cards unless they've first memorized basic strategy. This is

TABLE 12—Blackjack Side Bets

Game	Decks	Edge
Sweet 16	6	2.57%
21+3	2	2.78%
21+3	6	3.24%
Royal Match	1	3.77%
Pair Square	1	5.88%
Royal Match	6	6.67%
Over 13	1	6.79%
Under 13	1	10.11%
Pair Square	6	10.61%
Dare Any Pair	6	11.25%
Super Sevens	6	12.61%
Lucky Ladies (a)	6	24.71%
Bonus Blackjack	1	b
Bonus Blackjack	6	c

a: suited 20 pays 9 to 1
b: 22.78% less 3.77% per $100 in meter
c: 24.02% less 3.71% per $100 in meter

because the edge gained by counting is smaller than the edge lost by playing poorly. A player who attempts to count cards without first memorizing the basic strategy is making a costly mistake.

The theory behind card counting is that a deck rich in tens and aces is good for the player. When the portion of the deck remaining to be dealt is disproportionately rich in these good cards, the player should bet more, and sometimes make specific and calculated deviations from basic strategy. As cards are dealt, the counter keeps a running count of what has been played, which gives him information about what is left in the deck. Card counting is hard work and yields only about a 1%-1.5% edge under the best of conditions when done well. In addition, counters who are undercapitalized can easily lose their entire bankroll due to the inherent volatility of the game. If counting were an easy way to make money, everyone would be doing it. Recommended books on card counting can be found in Appendix H.

Spanish 21

Spanish 21 is a blackjack variant played with 48-card "Spanish" decks, which is a regular deck with the 10s removed. The removal of the 10s favors the dealer, but other rule changes favor the player. Depending on the specific rules, Spanish 21 is sometimes a better bet than conventional blackjack.

There are three versions of Spanish 21, differing only by two rules. The first rule variation is whether the dealer hits or stands on soft 17. The second rule variation is whether redoubling is allowed. Following is the house edge according to the disposition of these rules:

- Dealer hits soft 17, no redoubling: 0.76%
- Dealer stands on soft 17, no redoubling: 0.40%
- Dealer hits soft 17, redoubling allowed: 0.38%

Some casinos also offer a side bet that either or both of the player's first two cards will match the dealer's up-card. In a 6-deck game, a non-suited match pays 4-1 and a suited match pays 9-1. In an 8-deck game, a non-suited match pays 3-1 and a suited match pays 12-1. The side bet has a house edge of 3.06% in a 6-deck game and 2.99% in an 8-deck game.

Spanish 21 basic strategy is more complicated than conventional blackjack, because of the incentives to reach five cards and certain bonus hands. There's also much more hitting than conventional blackjack, because of the small-card-rich deck. Many players use conventional blackjack strategy in Spanish 21, but doing this increases the house edge by 0.48% if the dealer hits soft 17 and 0.53% if he stands. Don't be deterred from using the proper basic strategy. Basic strategy for all three Spanish 21 variations can be found in Appendix B.

If the strategy seems daunting, take heart: You can copy the tables and use them as a cheat sheet when you play at the table. I've used the printed strategy at the tables several times without incident.

Finally, never take insurance in this game. With the 10s removed from the deck, the insurance bet has a house edge of 24.7%.

Summary

In my opinion, blackjack is the best single game in the casino. Aside from bad games paying 6-5 on naturals, the house edge is always under 1% with the basic strategy. The game is interactive, fun to play, and has comparatively low volatility. Diligent players can also gain an advantage through card counting. If you play Spanish 21, be sure to use the proper basic strategy for that game.

5

Caribbean
Stud Poker

Caribbean Stud Poker is a poker-based table game in which each player plays only against the dealer, regardless of the number of players at the table. The game is easy to learn, large payoffs are possible, and near-perfect strategy can be mastered easily.

House Edge

Table 13 shows the house edge in Caribbean Stud following perfect strategy, as well as some alternative simplified strategies that are much easier to use.

TABLE 13—Caribbean Stud Edge vs. Different Strategies	
Strategy	**House edge**
Perfect strategy	5.224%
Basic strategy	5.225%
Raise with AKJ83 or better	5.316%
Raise with AK and match dealer up-card	5.334%

Variations

In most Caribbean Stud games, the royal flush pays 100-1. At the Star City casino in Australia, I saw a game with the royal flush paying 250 to 1, resulting in a slightly lower house edge of 5.20%. Many Internet casinos have different paytables, resulting in a house edge as low as 5.01% at casinos using Microgaming software.

Progressive-Jackpot Side Bet

In addition to the ante bet, you can also make a $1 side bet to win an extra bonus on hands of flush or better. This bet is based only on your own hand; the dealer's hand does not matter. About 71% of the money wagered on this side bet is added to a progressive meter and the casino keeps the rest. All player wins are paid directly out of the meter. When a player hits a royal flush, the casino replenishes the meter, usually with $10,000. At a 71% contribution rate and a meter re-seed of $10,000, the long-term house edge on the side bet is 27.46%.

Most players religiously make this side bet, worrying that if they get a great hand, they may win only their ante if the dealer doesn't qualify. While this is true, the fact remains that unless the meter reaches unusually high levels, the odds strongly favor the casino. Hence, this bet should almost always be avoided.

Of course, it's possible that the progressive meter could rise high enough to yield a positive-expectation wager. In the United States, the top prize of 100% of the meter amount is paid for a royal flush. A straight flush always pays 10% of the meter. The 4-of-a-kind, full house, and flush payouts vary from casino to casino. Table 14 lists six paytable variations that I've seen, along with information on the breakeven points for each.

The player's expected return is the amount in row 1 plus 2.92% for every $10,000 in the meter. Row 2 shows the amount needed for the side bet alone to have a 100% return, or no

TABLE 14—Caribbean Stud Progressive Jackpot

	Paytable 1	Paytable 2	Paytable 3	Paytable 4	Paytable 5	Paytable 6
4-of-a-kind	$100	$150	$500	$500	$500	$500
Full house	$75	$100	$100	$150	$75	$100
Flush pays	$50	$50	$50	$75	$50	$75

1) Return with $0 in meter

	23.03%	27.83%	36.24%	48.35%	32.64%	41.15%

2) Breakeven point for $1 side bet

	$263,205	$246,784	$218,047	$176,613	$230,363	$201,245

3) Breakeven point for $1 side bet and $5 base-game bet

	$352,533	$336,112	$307,375	$265,941	$319,691	$290,572

4) Breakeven point for $1 side bet and $10 base-game bet

	$441,860	$425,439	$396,702	$355,268	$409,018	$379,900

house edge. However, since you're required to make a wager on the base game in order to make the side bet, rows 3 and 4 of the table provide the practical information you need to determine when this bet becomes mathematically correct to make. These rows indicate the meter levels at which the advantage on the side bet exactly compensates for the house edge in the main game with minimum-bet requirements of $5 and $10, respectively.

The highest meter I've ever seen was $310,000 at the Claridge in Atlantic City. The game used paytable 3, so players had an advantage with a $5 bet. The casino raised the minimum to $10, and still players were standing around waiting to play.

Strategy

There are two simple strategy rules that cover 93.56% of all hands:

1. Always raise on a pair or higher.
2. Always fold with less than an ace and king.

Following are strategies that govern the play of the remaining ace/king hands.

Basic Strategy

The optimal strategy requires memorizing a table of 2,145 cells, one for each combination of the player's other three ranks across the dealer's up-card rank. Then there are 27 exceptions based on the way the cards are suited. Hence, there is the need for a simplified basic strategy that captures the lion's share of the gains from optimal play. The following basic strategy does this by telling you when to raise with an ace/king hand. If you memorize and play by these rules, the casino advantage is 5.23%, which compares favorably with the optimal strategy's 5.224%.

> Raise on ace and king if the dealer's up-card
> 1) is a queen or less and matches one of your cards.
> 2) is an ace or king and you have a queen or jack.
> 3) does not match any of your cards, you have a queen, and your fourth highest card is higher than the dealer's up-card.

It's good if one of your cards matches the dealer's up-card, because it lowers the probability that the dealer will pair up on that card to beat your ace/king. This strategy is so close to optimal that the player would have to play 444,478 hands before the expected costs due to inaccuracies in play reached the amount of a single bet.

Less-Accurate Strategies

If the basic strategy is too complicated, there are simpler strategies, which, of course, carry a higher house edge—but not much higher. For example, the difference between the basic strategy and the first strategy below is .11%, which amounts to about a half-penny in expected loss per $5 bet. The strategies are listed in house-edge order, from lowest to highest.

1) Raise with AKJ83 or better. According to the paper *An Analysis of Caribbean Stud Poker* by Peter Griffin and John Gwynn, Jr., this is the lowest hand in which the player should raise without considering the dealer's up-card. House edge: 5.32%.

2) Raise with AK and any card matching the dealer's up-card. House edge: 5.33%.

3) Raise with any pair or better. This is a risk-averse strategy, which may appeal to players who prefer not to raise in borderline situations. House edge: 5.47%.

4) Raise with any AK or better. This strategy may appeal to risk-takers who enjoy raising, even on borderline weak hands. House edge: 5.68%.

5) Raise on everything. This strategy, also known as "playing blind," is extremely ill-advised. The odds heavily favor folding on hands that do not qualify according to one of the criteria above. House edge: 16.61%.

Player Collusion

Although the rules forbid it, it's not unusual to see players flashing their cards to each other without the dealer taking steps to stop it. According to Griffin and Gwynn's *An Analysis of Caribbean Stud Poker* (which appears in the book *Finding the Edge*, edited by Olaf Vancura, William R. Eadington, and Judy A. Cornelius), in the perfect situation of having seven colluding players and a computer to make perfect use of all information obtained, the players would play with a 2.3% advantage. This is a big edge. The problem is, the use of computers is illegal in casinos and it would be difficult to feed all 35 cards held by the players into the computer in a timely fashion. So while the possibility exists, for practical purposes collusion will not result in a player advantage. However, in borderline ace/king hands there's value in peeking at other player hands. If you see other players' cards that match the dealer's up-card, there's greater reason to raise. It helps a little.

Summary

Learn when to raise with ace/king using one of the discussed strategies and avoid the side bet unless the progressive meter reaches the unusually high levels that have been identified.

6

Casino War

Casino War is without a doubt the easiest card game to play in the casino. If you ever played war as a child, Casino War will be instantly familiar. The player and dealer each get a card and the highest card wins. If each side gets the same card, then the player has the choice of surrendering or going to war. The posted rules are deceiving about this choice and are reminiscent of a carnival-game trick. They state that in a war, the player and dealer each match the original wager. Then both get a new card and the high card wins, with a second tie going to the player. The wording makes it sound as if the player has an advantage, because all appears equal except that the player wins on two consecutive ties. The catch is in the fact that when you go to war, the original bet only pushes if you win.

The alternative to going to war is to surrender half your bet. It's a less appealing option, because ties on a war go to the player. There's also a tie bet that pays 10 to 1.

Bonus Rules

Some casinos pay even money on both the first and second bets in the event of a second tie (after going to war). They may word it as getting a bonus, but it's the same as being paid even money on the entire wager. Note that outright winning war hands still push the first bet, which allows the house to retain an advantage.

House Edge

Table 15 shows the house edge for always going to war on ties with the bonus rules, always going to war on ties with regular rules, always surrendering on ties, and for the tie bet itself. Most casinos use 6 decks, but on the Internet, anything is possible.

TABLE 15—Casino War Edge by Number of Decks

Number of Decks	Go to War Bonus	Go to War No Bonus	Surrender	Tie Bet
1	2.06%	2.42%	2.94%	35.29%
2	2.24%	2.70%	3.40%	25.24%
3	2.29%	2.79%	3.55%	21.94%
4	2.31%	2.84%	3.62%	20.29%
5	2.32%	2.86%	3.67%	19.31%
6	2.33%	2.88%	3.70%	18.65%
7	2.34%	2.89%	3.72%	18.18%
8	2.34%	2.90%	3.73%	17.83%

Summary

Casino War has what looks like a reasonable house edge, but it plays extremely fast. Hence, your per-hour losses will be large. Look for casinos that offer the "bonus" rules and always go to war on ties.

7

Craps

Craps offers many bets, with the house edge ranging from 0.00% to 16.67%. It's important to know the house edge of each bet in order to avoid the sucker bets on this game that have high house edges. Table 16 on the following page lists the house edge for all the major bets on a crap table.

You may have seen the edge on the don't pass listed as 1.40%. This calculation is accurate assuming the player leaves his wager out until it wins or loses (playing past the tie when a 12 is rolled on the comeout). In the case of multiple-roll bets, such as buy and place, where the bet can be called off at any time, I assume that the player keeps his bet up until it wins or loses. Perfectionists have pointed out that if you make a place bet on 6 or 8 and leave it up just one roll, the house edge is only 0.46% counting ties.

Combining the Line Bets and Free Odds

While the odds bet is often referred to as "free odds" (because there is no house edge on the odds bet by itself), you must make the negative-expectation line bet before you can take or lay the odds. Table 17 on page 37 shows the combined house edge of the pass and don't pass bets coupled with the

TABLE 16—Crap Edge for Various Bets

Bet	House Edge
pass/come	1.41%
don't pass/don't come	1.36%
taking/laying odds	0.00%
place 4 or 10	6.67%
place 5 or 9	4.00%
place 6 or 8	1.52%
big 6 or 8	9.09%
buy all numbers	4.76%
(5% commission payable on all bets)	
buy 4 or 10	1.67%
(5% commission payable only on a win)	
lay 4 or 10	2.44%
lay 5 or 9	3.23%
lay 6 or 8	4.00%
craps 2/craps 12	13.89%
craps 3/yo 11	11.11%
any craps	11.11%
any 7	16.67%
field (12 pays 2-1)	5.56%
field (12 pays 3-1)	2.78%
hard 4 or 10	11.11%
hard 6 or 8	9.09%
horn	12.50%
horn, 2 or 12 high	12.78%
horn, 3 or 11 high	12.22%
world	13.33%

maximum odds bet allowed. The percentages indicate how much the long-term player can expect to lose as a fraction of total money bet (line bet and odds) in each situation.

TABLE 17—Crap Edge for Various Odds Multiples

Odds allowed	Pass	Don't Pass
1X	0.85%	0.68%
2X	0.57%	0.43%
Full double odds (a)	0.61%	0.45%
3X	0.47%	0.34%
3-4-5X (b)	0.37%	0.27%
5X	0.33%	0.23%
10X	0.18%	0.12%
20X	0.10%	0.06%
100X	0.02%	0.01%

(a) Full double odds: Player is allowed to take or lay 2.5X the line bet on points of 6 and 8, and 2X on all other points.

(b) 3/4/5X odds: Player may take or lay 3X the line bet on a point of 4 or 10, 4X on a 5 or 9, and 5X on a 6 or 8. Note that when taking the maximum odds, the win is always six times the line bet.

The best odds I have seen are 100X odds at the Casino Royale in Las Vegas. Over the years, other casinos, including Binion's Horseshoe, have offered 100X odds.

Players who wish to have their play on the crap table rated for comps should be warned that most casinos do not factor in the odds in measuring the average bet. However, a few do.

Crapless Craps

This is a crap variation that was developed at the old Vegas World in Las Vegas. It continues to be dealt at the casino's successor, the Stratosphere, and shows up from time to time in other places.

On the pass line bet, a 7 on the comeout roll still wins. Any other number becomes the point, including the 2, 3, 11, and 12. At first, this may seem like a positive change, because the player now has hope on the 2, 3, and 12 in exchange for giving up the sure winner on the 11. The problem is the 2, 3, and 12 will likely lose anyway, while the 11 changes from a winner to a likely loser. Overall, the house edge is 5.38% on the pass line, almost four times as high as conventional craps.

Fire Bet

A few casinos offer this bet, which wins if the shooter makes at least four different point numbers before sevening out. Only different point numbers count; if the player makes the same point twice, the second time does not count as a point made. Table 18 shows the probability for each number of points (as determined by random simulation), the payoff, and contribution to the total return. The house edge on this bet is 24.70%. Another fire bet paytable pays 25, 250, 1,000 for 4, 5 and 6, respectively, but on a *for-1* basis. That paytable has a house edge of 20.76%.

Strategy

I normally advise cutting down the house edge as much as possible. However, I wouldn't chastise anyone for betting the pass or come instead of the don't pass or don't come. The difference in the house edge is small and I think it's more fun to bet with the other players than against them. As long as

TABLE 18—Craps Fire Bet Probability and Edge

Points Made	Probability	Pays	Return
0	0.594522	-1	-0.594522
1	0.260503	-1	-0.260503
2	0.101038	-1	-0.101038
3	0.033364	-1	-0.033364
4	0.008776	10	0.087764
5	0.001633	200	0.326582
6	0.000164	2000	0.328063
Total	**1**		**-0.247017**

you stick to the line bets (pass, don't pass, come, don't come) and back them up with the odds, you'll be getting the best gambling deal available on a crap table.

I'm often asked how many come bets should be made after the pass line bet. Assuming the come bets are backed up with odds and left "working" during a comeout roll, there's no number that's better or worse than any other, so just do what you enjoy most. Note that you will increase your overall expectation marginally by keeping the come bet odds working during a comeout roll. Doing this lowers the combined house edge by 0.05% based on 5X odds.

Minimum-bet players who aren't comfortable making full-odds bets should not do so. Making the odds does not help you win more, it only helps you bet more at no additional cost. Betting in moderation is more important than betting correctly.

Never hedge bets in craps. In fact, you should never hedge your bets in any casino game, but this merits special mention in craps because so many players make this strategy mistake.

Players make hedge bets to "protect" one bet with another. For example, a hedge player might bet any craps on the comeout roll on the rationale that it will protect him if the shooter craps out. Or if the shooter makes a point, a hedge player might bet any seven to protect his pass line bet and odds against a seven-out. While making hedge bets can help minimize losses, they minimize wins much more. Despite what system salesmen would have you believe, there is no magic combination of bets in craps that will beat the house edge. When you mix high-house-edge bets with low-house-edge bets, regardless of the reason, it only increases the overall casino advantage. If you're tempted to make hedge bets because you're afraid of losing, then you probably shouldn't be gambling.

Long Hands and Hot Streaks

From time to time, casinos run "long-hand" promotions. For years, for example, Harold's Club in Reno had a long-hand meter that listed the longest rolls (without sevening out) over a given period of time. The California in Las Vegas has its Golden Arm Club, which enshrines the longest rollers. Once at the California, a player held the dice for 3 hours and 6 minutes. I don't know how many points he made, but Table 19 shows the probability of making various numbers of points (including repeating the same number) before sevening out.

TABLE 19—Probability of Points Before Seven Out

Points Made	Probability
5	1 in 91
10	1 in 8,205
15	1 in 743,254
20	1 in 67,326,003
25	1 in 6,098,577,369

Summary

To lower the house edge as much as possible, stick to the line bets (pass, come, don't pass, don't come) and use odds. Above all, avoid hedging and the high-edge proposition bets.

8

Keno

Although live keno carries one the highest house edges of all casino games, it's played at a very slow pace and you can bet as little as $1 per game. So if you have a limited budget and are looking for a way to kill some time before the bus takes you home, keno might be a good choice.

To illustrate the odds of a typical game, Table 20 shows the probability of catching 0 to 9 numbers on a common pay-table for a 9-spot ticket and the contribution to the total return. The total return shows that the player can expect to get back 70.23% per dollar bet on average for a house edge of

TABLE 20—Keno Probability and Edge (9-Spot)

Matches	Probability	Pays	Return
0	0.063748	0	0.000000
1	0.220666	0	0.000000
2	0.316426	0	0.000000
3	0.246109	0	0.000000
4	0.114105	0	0.000000
5	0.032601	4	0.130406
6	0.005720	43	0.245941
7	0.000592	300	0.177504
8	0.000033	4000	0.130370
9	0.000001	25000	0.018107
Total	**1.000000**		**0.702327**

29.77%. This is a representative percentage for a keno game; however, there's a fair amount of variation in games. Appendix C shows a list comparing 9-spots at 37 casinos in Las Vegas, with returns varying from 66.24% (Palms) to 79.85% (Silverton). Also, returns in various keno games are not uniform. For example, the *Las Vegas Advisor* newsletter recently reported a $1.10 7-spot ticket at the El Cortez in downtown Las Vegas that returned 90.4% and Fitzgeralds had a $10 8-spot returning 95.3%. Novelty games, such as all-or-nothing tickets, tend to have lower returns.

Progressive Keno

Most casinos that offer progressive keno put a cap on the jackpots, preventing the games from ever coming close to offering a positive-expectation bet. However, there are a few uncapped progressive keno games at any given time in Nevada casinos (the Gold Coast, Orleans, and Fremont in Las Vegas have each had one for years).

Whenever a progressive exists, there's a number at which the game's return goes positive. At the time of this writing, the Orleans in Las Vegas has a progressive on its $2 8- and 9-spots, which share the same jackpot. The jackpot is six times easier to hit on the 8-spot, so that's what the player should play. The general formula for calculating the return for this 8-spot is 50.97% plus 2.17% for each $10,000 in the meter. Hence, at a meter of $225,650.75, the expected value of the 8-spot goes positive. I've heard of five progressive winners on this game, all with 8-spot tickets. The winning meters have been $185,317.09, $106,373.66, $172,616.09, $118,454.00, and $160,380.48—all below the positive level. Even though it's unlikely that the meter will rise high enough without being hit to surpass the breakeven point, it's not rare for it to rise high enough to become one of the best keno games in Las Vegas.

Looking at Appendix C, you can see that the best fixed-odds game at the Silverton returns 79.85%. For the Orleans to surpass this return, the meter need only pass $132,907.56, which it often does. The process for deriving the expected return on the Orleans' progressive 8-spot is to begin with a base return of 50.96% (based on returns for a $2 ticket paying $10 for 5 numbers, $150 for 6 numbers, and $3,000 for 7 numbers), then add 2.17% for each $10,000 on the meter.

Taxation of Winnings

Casinos require that you fill out a W-2G form for net winnings at keno of $1,500 or more. Unlike slot winnings, you can deduct the cost of the ticket. For example, catching 7 out of 8 on a $1 ticket at the Luxor returns $1,500. However the net win is $1,500-$1 = $1,499 and does not necessitate a W-2G.

Video Keno

The good news about video keno is that returns are much higher than live keno—usually 85% to 95% (the exception is the 1-spot, which invariably pays 3-for-1, for a return of 75%). The bad news is that you can play the video version several times as fast as live keno, so expected losses per hour can easily be greater than lounge keno, depending on bet size and playing speed.

In January 2004 I sampled a dozen 25¢ 8-spots in Reno and Lake Tahoe. Table 21 on the following page shows the returns in this sampling.

The table shows a fairly tight grouping between 92.31% and 94.90%. Of the 12 casinos surveyed, there were only three different paytables. Aside from the game at the Sands Regency, the only difference in the table was for catching 5 numbers, where one paytable paid 12 and the other 13. Some casinos paid slightly more for the higher coin-denomination machines, but most had the same paytable across all denominations.

TABLE 21—Returns for 25¢ Video Keno (8-Spot) in Reno/Lake Tahoe

Casino	Return
Fitzgeralds	94.90%
Virginian	94.90%
Cal-Neva	94.90%
Peppermill	94.90%
John Ascuaga's Nugget	94.90%
Lakeside Inn	94.90%
Atlantis	94.90%
Sands Regency	92.62%
Eldorado	92.31%
Silver Legacy	92.31%
Circus Circus	92.31%
Horizon	92.31%

Caveman Keno

IGT offers a variation called Caveman Keno on its Game King machines. In Caveman Keno, the computer picks three dinosaur eggs among the numbers not chosen by the player. If any of the 20 randomly drawn numbers match an egg number, that egg hatches and the player's winnings are multiplied by the number of eggs that hatch. For zero or one egg, the factor is 1. For two eggs, it's 4. And for three eggs it's 10. The return on Caveman Keno is about the same as the conventional keno game offered on the same machine, about 92%-94%.

Strategy

There is no strategy for picking winning numbers in keno. It doesn't help to study which numbers have hit in the past. It also doesn't help to play fancy combination tickets. It does matter to some degree how many numbers are picked, but not which ones specifically. I've been asked many times if the odds of winning with 1, 2, 3, 4, 5, 6 are the same as with six random numbers in keno or the lottery. The answer is the odds are exactly the same.

In a lottery there's a slight value in picking non-popular sets of numbers, which lessens the chance that you'll have to split the jackpot if you win. Due to the far fewer players participating at any given time, this strategy is not important when playing keno.

The Worst Bet in Vegas

As far as I know, the worst bet in Las Vegas (outside of some obscure sports bets) is "Millionaire Keno," offered at Harrah's and Rio. The expected return is 39.99%, which means the house edge is over 60%! Not far behind is "Million Dollar Keno" at the Las Vegas Hilton with a return of 43.05%.

Summary

It's not which numbers you pick, it's where you play that matters. Video keno usually has a much higher return than live keno, but is also much faster paced. If you must play keno, I recommend going "low and slow." In video keno, find a nickel machine and play one coin per game. In live keno, play the $1 or lower tickets (the expected losses for these two approaches are similar. Also look for progressive meters that might be approaching, or even above, breakeven.

9

Let It Ride

Let It Ride is one of the more successful new casino games. It's easy to play, offers the potential for big payoffs, and allows players to exercise strategy. Unlike other poker-based table games, there's no dealer hand; the player's results are based entirely on his own hand. Let It Ride is played like five-card stud in reverse. Instead of adding to your bet as cards are revealed, you are allowed to pull back parts of the bet if the odds don't look promising. Table 22 shows the paytable. The only exception to this paytable is in video Let It Ride, which is addressed later.

TABLE 22—Let It Ride Paytable

Hand	Payoff
Royal flush	1,000 to 1
Straight flush	200 to 1
4-of-a-kind	50 to 1
Full house	11 to 1
Flush	8 to 1
Straight	5 to 1
3-of-a-kind	3 to 1
Two pair	2 to 1
Tens or better	1 to 1

House Edge

The house edge in Let It Ride, defined as the ratio of the expected loss to one of the original three wagers, is 3.51%.

Strategy

The following rules indicate when to "let it ride." Since the minimum paying hand is a pair of 10s, a "high card" is a 10 or greater.

Let it ride with three cards with:

• Any paying hand (pair of 10s or better).
• Any three to a royal flush.
• Three suited cards in a row, except A23 and 234.
• Three to a straight flush, with one gap, with at least one high card.
• Three to a straight flush, with two gaps, with at least two high cards.

Let it ride with four cards with:

• Any paying hand (pair of 10s or better).
• Any four to a flush (including straight and royal flush).
• Any four to an open-end straight with at least one high card.
• Any four to an open-end straight with zero high cards (a borderline play with zero house edge).
• Any four to an inside straight with 4 high cards. (A borderline play with zero house edge.)

Player Collusion

As in Caribbean Stud, players are not supposed to share information, but they often do. It's not unusual, for example, to see players showing each other their cards. This may be helpful with the 4-card zero-house-edge hands. If you see the cards you need, then pull back a bet. The benefit of doing this is likely small.

Progressive Side Bet

Most casinos offer a $1 side bet, which pays based on the final 5-card hand. Side bets in any game almost always carry a higher house edge than the game itself and Let It Ride is no exception. In my travels, I've seen eight different paytables for this side bet, ranging in house edge from 13.77% (only once at the Lady Luck in Las Vegas) to 36.52% (seen at New York-New York). Table 23 shows the returns for all eight paytables. The bottom row is the house edge that corresponds to that paytable. The house edge on all of them is high. Hence, I recommend avoiding it.

TABLE 23—Let It Ride Progressive Returns

Hand	Paytables							
	1	2	3	4	5	6	7	8
Royal flush	20000	20000	20000	20000	20000	10000	20000	20000
Straight flush	2000	1000	2000	2000	1000	2000	2000	1000
4-of-a-kind	100	100	100	400	400	100	300	300
Full house	75	75	75	200	200	75	150	150
Flush	50	50	50	50	50	50	50	50
Straight	25	25	25	25	25	25	25	25
3-of-a-kind	9	4	8	5	5	8	5	5
Two pair	6	3	4	0	0	4	0	0
High pair	0	1	0	0	0	0	0	0
House edge	13.77%	23.73%	25.39%	25.53%	26.92%	26.93%	35.14%	36.52%

Video Let It Ride

Don't be fooled by the paytable in video Let It Ride. All the pays on a full house or less are 1 more than the table game. However, as is the case with all machine games, the original bet is not returned. To compare apples to apples, you must subtract one from each number. This results in standard pay-offs up to 4-of-a-kind, after which the return is one coin less than standard. This increases the house edge to 3.57%. However, the cashback and comp points you earn playing the machines at most casinos are likely worth much more than the 0.06% you give up on these paytables. Also, remember that the number of hands per hour is much more than a live game. So I would recommend lowering your bet when playing the video version.

Summary

If poker variations are your cup of tea, you may enjoy Let It Ride. However, for the gambler looking for a good bet, Let It Ride, like most of the newer games, does not compete well against the old classics. If you must play, the strategy in this chapter is not difficult to learn and will allow you to play perfectly. Finally, above all, avoid the side bet.

10

Pai Gow Poker

Pai gow poker is based on the ancient Chinese domino game of pai gow. Instead of using dominos, pai gow poker uses playing cards. To avoid the common confusion between the two games, the card game should always be referred to as pai gow poker and not simply pai gow. Pai gow poker is a good game for bankroll preservation: The house edge is low, the pace is slow, and volatility is low because many hands result in a push as shown in Table 24, which lists the possible outcomes of a bet in pai gow poker assuming both player and dealer are following the same "house way."

TABLE 24—Pai Gow Poker Possible Outcomes

Outcome	Probability
Player wins both	28.61%
Banker wins both	29.91%
Tie	41.48%

House Edge

The preceding table shows that the probability of a win is 1.3% higher as the banker than as the player. The reason for this is that the banker wins on "copies" (hands with the exact same value). The probability of a copy is 2.55% on the front hand and 0.32% on the back hand. You must win both the front and the back hand to win your bet (and a 5% commission is retained by the house) or lose both hands to lose the bet. Table 25 shows the house edge in a one-on-one game against a player when acting as player or banker, assuming both parties are following the same house way.

TABLE 25—Pai Gow Poker Edge for Single Player vs. Dealer

Side	House Edge
Player	2.73%
Banker	0.20%

The news gets even better for the banker as the number of players increases, because the 5% commission on winnings is charged on the net win as banker, rather than on a hand-by-hand basis. Table 26 shows the house edge as banker according to the number of other players, assuming all other players (including the dealer) are betting the same amount and all follow the same house way.

TABLE 26—Pai Gow Poker Edge as Banker

Other Players (including dealer)	House Edge
1	+0.20%
2	-0.02%
3	-0.10%
4	-0.15%
5	-0.19%
6	-0.21%

Table 26 shows that it takes only two other participants to swing the odds in the banker's favor for that hand. Assuming you are willing to bank, the overall house edge will depend on various factors, including the number of players, how much the other players bet, how little you must bet as the player, how often you get a turn to bank, how skillful you are in setting your hands, and how unskillful your opponents are. Watch out for tables where the turn to bank zig-zags between each player in turn and the dealer. If you want to bank, look for a table where the turn rotates around the table and skips players who choose not to bank. Better yet, look for tables where if a player declines to bank, the option goes to the next player in that same turn. In games like this, you can bank every other hand regardless of the number of players, as long as they opt not to bank. Fortunately, in this situation other players rarely opt to bank.

Of course, all this information about player banking is academic if you aren't comfortable banking because the other players are betting too much. Overbetting your bankroll is a serious mistake in any game and you shouldn't bank if you aren't comfortable with assuming the responsibility of paying the winners if you lose.

Strategy

More important than setting your cards perfectly is how much of the action you bank. It's advantageous to be the banker for two reasons: 1) You win on matching hands ("copies"), and 2) the 5% commission is charged only on the net win, not each individual win.

With regard to playing strategy, there is no easy rule of thumb that explains how to set any hand. Optimal strategy is extremely complicated and I doubt that anyone knows it completely. However, the casino house ways, which vary slightly from one to another, are good solid strategies (see Appendix D for an example of house-way strategy).

The Wizard's Two-Pair Rule

The proper play of two pair is complicated. Here's an easy-to-remember strategy that's also more powerful than the conventional house way. Consider the point value of each pair's rank as it corresponds to the poker value — a pair of 5s is 5 points, a pair of 8s is 8 points, a pair of queens is 12 points, etc. Simply add the point value of each pair. For example, a two pair of 5s and 7s would have a total point value of 12. The rule is to always split the two pair unless:

1) The total point value is 9 or less and you have a king or ace singleton, or
2) The total point value is 15 or less and you have an ace singleton.

According to my calculations, following this advice will increase the expected return by 0.04% above the conventional two-pair-rule house way.

Fortune Pai Gow Poker

Fortune pai gow poker is ordinary pai gow poker with an optional side bet. The side bet pays on the make-up of the player's seven cards, regardless of how the hand is set. There's also an "envy bonus" if one of the other players gets at least a 4-of-a-kind, whether or not the other player made the Fortune side bet. The player must bet at least $5 on the side bet to qualify for the envy bonus.

Table 27 shows the return for this side bet. The house edge is 5.85%, before considering the envy bonuses.

For every other player seated at the table the house edge is reduced by 0.93%. Table 28 shows the house edge after considering the envy bonus according to the number of other players at the table (not including yourself).

TABLE 27—Fortune Pai Gow Poker Side Bet Return

Hand	Pays	Probability	Inverse Probability	Return
Natural 7-card straight flush	8000 to 1	0.00000021	1 in 4761905	0.001661
Royal flush plus royal match	2000 to 1	0.00000062	1 in 1612903	0.001246
Wild 7-card straight flush	1000 to 1	0.00000127	1 in 787402	0.001272
Five aces	400 to 1	0.00000732	1 in 136612	0.002927
Royal flush	150 to 1	0.00016865	1 in 5929	0.025297
Straight flush	50 to 1	0.00119787	1 in 835	0.059894
4-of-a-kind	25 to 1	0.00199472	1 in 501	0.049868
Full house	5 to 1	0.02717299	1 in 37	0.135865
Flush	4 to 1	0.04004129	1 in 25	0.160165
3-of-a-kind	3 to 1	0.04977518	1 in 20	0.149326
Straight	2 to 1	0.07788883	1 in 13	0.155778
Other	no pay	0.80175105	1 in 1	-0.80175
Total		**1**		**-0.05845**

TABLE 28—Fortune Pai Gow Poker Edge by Players

Other Players	House Edge
0	5.85%
1	4.92%
2	3.99%
3	3.06%
4	2.13%
5	1.20%

Progressive Pai Gow Poker

Some games offer a $1 side bet that pays according to a separate progressive meter for each of five winning hands. The meter contribution rates change depending on how much money has gone through since the last jackpot hand of five aces. According to game literature from the manufacturers, the overall house edge is 42%. The casino operator can also choose how high it reseeds the meters when someone wins, which also affects the house edge.

However, most important to the player is how high the meters are at the time of play. Table 29 shows the probability of drawing each of the five winning hands. To determine your expected return, multiply the probability of each hand by what it pays at the time. Given the high average house edge, the odds rarely swing to the player's advantage; in a small sampling of five tables I conducted, the house edge was 51.4%.

TABLE 29—Progressive Pai Gow Poker Probability

Hand	Probability
Five aces	0.00000732
Natural royal flush	0.00002927
Wild royal flush	0.00014026
Straight flush	0.00119909
4-of-a-kind	0.00199472
All other	0.99662934

No Push Pai Gow Poker

Another variation of pai gow poker called "No Push Pai Gow Poker" has the same rules as regular pai gow poker except:

• The dealer is always the banker.
• No commission is charged on winners.
• After all hands are dealt, the next two cards are set aside to break ties, one card for all players collectively and one card for the dealer. If the players' card is highest, all players win

on the tie. If the dealer's card is greater or equal, the dealer wins the tie.

The house edge under these rules is 3.90%, which is greater than conventional pai gow poker even if the player never banks.

California Rules

There are several card rooms in the Los Angeles area where pai gow poker is legal. In these clubs, the dealer never banks, but simply provides the service of dealing the cards. There's also no 5% commission on winnings, but dealers take a rake out of every pot. For large bettors, the rake often works out to less than a 5% commission. This can result in a strong player advantage if the other players are averse to banking. For more information on California pai gow poker, I recommend *Optimal Strategy for Pai Gow Poker* by Stanford Wong.

Summary

Act as banker as often as you can if you are comfortable with the risk. The house edge is higher when not banking, so bet less at those times. Follow my two-pair rule for splitting a two pair, otherwise it's hard to play better than the house way. Serious players should consider playing in the Los Angeles-area card clubs.

11

Racetrack Betting

While this chapter discusses horse racing, the same principles apply in dog racing. My objective is to explain the various betting options available, show how the odds are calculated, and relate the house advantage. I won't offer advice on how to choose the right horse to bet on, since that is a complicated and subjective topic that requires skills in "handicapping." This chapter is written to make the random or casual picker more informed about the betting options.

All racetracks operate on what is called a pari-mutuel basis. This means that player bets are pooled, the track takes out a certain percentage for expenses and profit, and the rest is returned to the winners. The portion of the pool the racetrack deducts is called the "takeout," which is roughly equivalent mathematically to the house edge in traditional gambling games. It's important to understand that the bettors are not betting against the track, but against each other. Unlike sports betting, where the payoffs are locked in at the moment a bet is made, payoffs at the track are in constant flux, depending on the demand for each bet. Only after the race is over, the results certified, and the math calculated will the payoffs be posted. That is one of the exciting aspects of racetrack betting: knowing your horse has won, but waiting to see what your winning ticket is worth.

Betting Options

There are many different bets available at the track. The most basic (and popular) are the win, place, and show bets. These are simple bets involving only one horse and one race. All other bets, known as "exotics," involve picking multiple horses and pay long odds. The win, place, and show bets have a lower takeout than the exotics and, thus, are the better bets to make. Following is a list of the major bets available.

Win: A bet that a chosen horse will finish in first place.

Place: A bet that a chosen horse will finish in first or second place.

Show: A bet that a chosen horse will finish in first, second, or third place.

Daily Double: A bet on the first-place horse in two consecutive races, generally the first two races.

Daily Triple/Pick Three: A bet on picking the first-place horse in three consecutive races.

Exacta: A bet on the first- and second-place horses in a single race; must specify the exact order.

Quinella: A bet on the first- and second-place horses in a single race finishing in any order.

Trifecta: A bet on the first-, second-, and third-place horses in a single race; must specify the exact order.

Twin Trifecta: This is a pair of trifecta bets on two races. The winning pool is split between the winners of the first trifecta and winners of both of them.

Superfecta: A bet on the first-, second-, third-, and fourth-place horses in a single race; must specify the exact order.

Odd/Even: A bet based on whether the number of the winning horse is odd or even.

Pick Six: A bet on the first-place horse in six consecutive races, generally the last six. In the event no one wins, the pool is divided between those correctly picking five (or four if nobody picks five) and a "carryover," which goes into the next pick-six pool. The pick six can be an attractive bet after a carryover, possibly resulting in a player advantage, depending in large part on pick-six demand the following day (which tends to increase if there is a carryover).

To place a bet at the racetrack, you must first know exactly what you want to bet and how much. There's usually a line at the betting window, where there's often little patience for indecision. The minimum bet is usually $2 on win, place, and show bets and $1 on all others. There's a specific way to make a wager at the betting window. The bettor should state, in order, the amount bet, the horse number, the type of wager, and the race number. For example, you might say "$2 on number 5 to place in the third race." If you're betting at a remote location that services multiple racetracks, you should state which track you're betting at first.

About a minute after the end of the race the tote board will display the value of winning win, place, and show tickets relative to a $2 wager, similar to the example in Table 30.

TABLE 30—Sample Tote-Board Display

	Horse	Win	Place	Show
1st	5	7.00	3.00	2.70
2nd	2		2.40	2.20
3rd	3			3.50

These amounts include the original $2 wager. For example, a $2 place bet on horse 5 would pay $3.00 ($1.00 in winnings and $2.00 for the return of the original wager). The tote board will also display what the winning exotic bets pay. All winning tickets are paid at the same odds as a $2 ticket. In the above example, a winning $50 show bet on horse 5 would be worth $67.50 (25 times the $2 payout of $2.70).

House Edge

The house edge is mostly a function of the track take-out, but it's also affected by the breakage, whether the track rounds to 10¢ or 20¢. In general, the win, place, and show bets have the lowest takeout. The two-horse picks, such as daily doubles, quinellas, and exactas, are higher. Longshots, such as the trifecta and pick six, have the highest takeout.

Table 31 shows the takeout for various tracks around the United States. It's delineated by track; state is indicated because all tracks in the same state will usually have the same takeout percentage. This information was taken from and can be found at the Web site of the *Daily Racing Form*.

Payoff Calculation

Each classification of bet has a separate pool of money. For example, all place bets are combined in one pool, regardless of which horses are bet. Winnings are calculated as follows, based on each individual pool.

1. The track's takeout is deducted from the total pool.
2. Total bets made by winners, which are refunded, are deducted from the pool. The amount remaining in the pool is available to pay as winnings.
3. If there are multiple winning horses, the remaining pool is divided by the number of winners. For example, a show-bet pool would be divided by three to create three sub-pools, one for each horse finishing in the top three.
4. Each sub-pool is divided by the total amount bet on that horse. This is the ratio of winnings per money bet.
5. Each ratio from step 4 is multiplied by $2, then

TABLE 31—Takeout at Various Racetracks

Track	State	Win/ place/show	2 horse picks1	3+ horse picks2
Prescott Downs	AZ	18.5%	22.5%	22.5%
Oak Lawn	AR	17%	21%	21%
Hollywood Park	CA	15.43%	20.18%	20.18%
Arapahoe Park	CO	18.5%	25%	25%
Delaware Park	DE	17%	19%	25%
Tampa Bay Downs	FL	18.9%	25.9%	25.9%
Les Bois Park	ID	18%	22.75%	24.75%
Arlington Park	IL	17%	20.5%	25%
Prairie Meadows	IA	18%	24%	25%
Churchill Downs	KY	16%	19%	19%
Delta Downs	LA	17%	20.5%	25%
Laurel	MD	17%	19%	25%
Great Lakes Downs	MI	17%	20.5%	20.5%
Fonner Park	NE	15%	23%	23%
Meadowlands	NJ	17%	19%	25%
The Downs	NM	22%	22%	25%
Aqueduct	NY	15%	20%	25%
River Downs	OH	18%	22%	22%
Remington Park	OK	18%	20%	20%
Portland Meadows	OR	18%	22%	22%
Philadelphia Park	PA	17%	20%	30%
Lone Star	TX	18%	21%	25%
Colonial Downs	VA	18%	22%	22%
Emerald Downs	WA	15.1%	22.1%	22.1%
Charles Town	WV	17.3%	19%	25%

1. *2 horse picks refers to daily doubles, quinellas, and exactas.*
2. *3+ horse picks refers to trifectas, pick 6, and other longshots.*
3. *Takeout for odd/even bet is 5% at Churchill Downs.*
4. *Takeout for pick 3 is 25% at Great Lakes Downs.*
5. *Takeout for pick 3 is 26% at Philadelphia Park.*

rounded down to a multiple of 10¢ or 20¢. This rounding down is the breakage.

6. The sum of the winnings in step 5 and $2 is taken. This is the total amount payable for a winning $2 ticket. Larger bets are paid at the same odds as a winning $2 ticket.

Here are some examples. First, consider a simple win bet. Assume that $1,000 is bet in total on win bets by all bettors, $200 is bet on the winning horse by all bettors, and the track's takeout is 17%. After the takeout, there will be $830 left. Then the $200 bet on the winner is deducted, which leaves $630 to pay as winnings. The ratio of winnings to money bet on the winner is $630/$200 = 3.15. The product of 3.15 and $2 is $6.30. This amount gets rounded down to $6.20. So a winning $2 ticket is worth $8.20 ($6.20 in winnings plus the original $2 bet).

In this example, if the bettor made a larger bet—for example, $50—it would be paid at the same odds as a $2 ticket. In this case the ratio of the return to the original wager is $8.20/$2.00 = 4.1, so a $50 winning ticket would be worth $50 x 4.1 = $205.

Next consider a place-bet pool. For example, assume $1,000 is bet on place bets and the first- and second-place horses are 6 and 8. Further assume $100 is bet on horse 6 and $200 is bet on horse 8. First, the track takes its 17% cut, leaving $830. Then winning bets of $300 are deducted, leaving $530 to pay the winners. Half of the $530 ($265) will be paid to the winners on each horse. In this case the ratio of winnings to winning bets will be $265/$100 = 2.65 on horse 6 and $265/$200 = 1.325 on horse 8. The unrounded return for a $2 bet is 2.65 x $2 = $5.30 on horse 6 and 1.325 x $2 = $2.65 on horse 8. These amounts are rounded to $5.20 and $2.60, respectively. Including the original wager, winning $2 place tickets receive $7.20 on horse 6 and $4.60 on horse 8.

Sometimes when a strong favorite wins, especially on a show bet, the winnings may round down to nothing. In this event the track must pay back a minimum of $2.10 per $2.00 bet. The track is allowed to take from the other pools on the same type of bet when this occurs.

Distorted Show Pools

A winning ticket must pay at least 5% in winnings, or $2.10 on a $2.00 ticket. Sometimes when a race has a small number of horses and a huge favorite, there's a player advantage for betting the favorite to show. In fact, if the probability of the favorite showing is at least 95.24%, then the show bet has an advantage.

Sometimes when this situation occurs and the favorite does not show, the winning show bets pay more than win and place bets. This happened in the 8th race at Laurel Park on December 31, 2003. Bettors bet $51,733 on Richetta, a 2-5 favorite, to show. In this race the total show pool was $55,593, so the favorite captured 93.06% of the show pool. When Richetta finished sixth, there was a lot of money to divide among those who bet the other 6.94% on the first three place horses to show ("bridge jumpers" is the term for those who bet a huge favorite to show, because when they lose they feel like jumping off a bridge). The results of this race are shown in Table 32.

TABLE 32—Tote Board for a Distorted Show Pool

#	Horse	Jockey	Win	Place	Show
2	Pour It On	Rodriguez E D	74.20	25.20	99.20
5	Sea of Promises	Hutton G W		6.80	30.00
1	Grant's Moon	Pino M G			38.00

Source: Baltimore Sun, January 1, 2004

Taxation of Winnings

Some bizarre rules determine when the track reports your winnings to the IRS or deducts taxes directly. If a ticket pays 300-1 or more and totals more than $600, gambling-revenue form W-2G will be generated and reported to the IRS. If a ticket pays 300-1 or more and pays more than $5,000, 28% will automatically be withheld for income taxes. Some states take out state taxes on top of that. Some players try to break large long-shot wagers into smaller bets to skirt the withholding rules. Careful with this, as it could be construed as a form of tax evasion.

Off-Track Betting

If you can't make it to the track, there are other ways of making a wager on a race. Most Nevada casinos offer over-the-counter bets on horse races in their race books. The race books tie into the betting pools at the track, so financially speaking, it's as if you are actually betting at the track. For this reason, racetrack betting is the only bet you can make in a casino in which the casino is truly on your side. It's simply offering a service, for which it gets a cut of the track's share of the pool.

Some states have off-track sites ("OTBs") where you can make a wager, but must pay an additional fee. In Oregon, for example, a 5% surcharge is added to each bet made at an OTB. In Tijuana, 1% of winning wagers (on both horses and sports) is retained by the betting parlors. Some services accept bets over the phone, usually charging a fee per day or per call.

Summary

Stick to the win, place, and show bets and avoid the exotics. If given the choice, wager at tracks with the lowest takeout percentages.

12

Roulette

Roulette should need little introduction. It's a simple game of luck that any 10-year-old could understand and play. Two important rule variations can greatly affect the house edge.

• *Number of zeros* – In almost all cases, there are either one or two (though there are instances of games with more).
• *Half-back* – In some variations, if the ball lands on zero or double zero the player loses only half his wager on even-money bets.

Table 33 shows the house edge based on all four combinations of the above two rules.

TABLE 33—Roulette Edge

Single zero	Half back	Even Money Bets	All Other Bets
Yes	Yes	1.35%	2.70%
Yes	No	2.70%	2.70%
No	Yes	2.63%	5.26%*
No	No	5.26%	5.26%*

* House edge on 5-number combination bet is 7.89%

European roulette wheels generally feature just one zero, plus the half-back rule on even-money bets (often known as "en prison"), or some variation. Following are some specific rules I've seen or heard of.

Berlin – If the ball lands on zero, all even-money bets are "imprisoned." The next spin is used to resolve the bet. If the next spin results in a win, the bet is released and returned to the player without winnings. Otherwise the bet is lost, including on a subsequent zero. This results in a house edge of 1.39% on even-money bets.

Holland – Same rule as Berlin, except if zero is hit on two consecutive spins, the bet becomes double imprisoned. In this case two consecutive wins are necessary to release the bet. Any further zeros result in a loss. This results in a house edge of 1.37% on even-money bets.

Hamburg – If the ball lands on zero, half of all even-money bets are returned. This results in a house edge of 1.35%.

Games with more than two zeros are not unknown and should be avoided.

Good-Game Locations

Most roulette games in the United States feature the unfavorable double zeros and no half-back on losses. However, there are exceptions. In Atlantic City, the double-zero wheels feature the half-back rule. There are also plenty of single-zero wheels in Atlantic City, but they don't feature the half-back rule. Las Vegas has several single-zero wheels around town, often with high minimums (but not always; Nevada Palace and Stratosphere have run low-minimum single-zero games for several years now). The Grand in Tunica also features a single-zero wheel.

The best rules can be found at select high-end Las Vegas casinos (e.g., Bellagio, Mirage, and Aladdin), which offer single-zero roulette with the half-back rule.

Strategy

The only strategy in roulette is finding wheels with favorable rules. Most important is to play single zeros rather than double zeros when possible. This may sound obvious, but on occasions where both are available side by side, players will usually be split between them, the double-zero players oblivious to the fact that the casino edge is cut almost in half just a couple steps away. If the half-back rule is in force, make even-money bets only. Always stay away from the 5-number combination bet offered in double-zero roulette. Otherwise, there is no strategy in predicting numbers, bet size, or bet placement. You may as well fly by the seat of your pants.

Betting Systems

Contrary to popular belief among roulette players, no event (number, color, column, etc.) in roulette is ever overdue. It doesn't matter how many times in a row the ball has landed on red; the odds of a red on the next spin are always equal to those of black. Roulette has been around for some 300 years and throughout its history, players have searched for a way to overcome the house edge. Some players believe (incorrectly) that the odds favor numbers that are overdue to hit. Others believe (incorrectly) that methods of bet-size variation can cause wins to exceed losses. It's mathematically impossible to gain an advantage over a fair game of roulette. No one has ever done so and no one ever will. The *Encyclopædia Britannica* recognizes the futility as follows:

"The oldest and most common betting system is the Martingale or 'doubling-up' system, in which bets are doubled progressively. This probably dates back to the invention of the Roulette wheel, but every day of the week some gambler somewhere reinvents it, or some variation of it, and believes he has something new. Over the years hundreds of 'sure-fire' winning systems have been dreamed up, but regardless of what system is used, in the long run it cannot overcome the house's advantage of the 0, or 0 and 00. This house advantage is the only system that consistently wins in the long run."

Dealer Signature and Biased Wheels

I've been asked on numerous occasions about the effectiveness of wheel tracking. Believers in a theory known as "dealer signature" maintain that, due to muscle memory, roulette dealers spin the ball at the same speed every time. Thus, they believe the player can predict where the ball will land according to the wheel's position at the time of ball release. I'm very skeptical that the human eye is precise enough to accomplish this and have seen no evidence that it has ever been done successfully. No credible gambling writer that I know of has endorsed this as a viable way to beat roulette.

On the other hand, roulette is known to have been beaten by exploiting biased wheels and with computer-aided prediction. The former involves finding a wheel with a pronounced mechanical deficiency that favors certain numbers. The latter involves using (hidden) modern technology to ascertain wheel speed, ball speed, and ball position to predict at least what part of the wheel the ball will land in. In 2004, a team in London using laser scanners and microcomputers was believed to have won 1.3£ million with roulette prediction before being caught. (Before you get excited, using a "device" to gamble in Nevada is a felony.)

Summary

As in keno, it isn't the numbers you bet on that matter, but where you play. Look for wheels with a single zero, or half back on losses if the ball lands on a zero, or better yet, both.

13

Sic Bo

Sic Bo is probably the least popular game in this book. It's often found in Asian game rooms, such as those in Atlantic City. Some of the larger Las Vegas casinos may have a table, but often with restricted hours. If you can't find the game it's just as well, since most of the bets carry a very high house edge.

Sic Bo is based on an ancient Chinese dice game (the name is Chinese for "dice pair"). It's played on a large table with a host of bets to choose from and uses three dice and a dice shaker. Players may bet on as many of the available wagers as they like. Once betting is closed, the dealer shakes the dice, opens the shaker, and lights up all winning bets on the table according to the combinations that come up on the dice.

Payoffs can vary from one casino to another. Table 34 shows the payoffs currently in use in all Atlantic City casinos and in some casinos in Las Vegas. It's not unusual to find games that pay less on these propositions, which increases the odds against the player.

TABLE 34—Sic Bo Probabilities and Edge

Bet Name	Wins on	Probability of Winning	Pays	House Edge
Small	Total of 4-10, except for a 3-of-a-kind	48.61%	1 to 1	2.78%
Big	Total of 11-18, except for 3-of-a-kind	48.61%	1 to 1	2.78%
4	Total of 4	1.39%	60 to 1	15.28%
5	Total of 5	2.78%	30 to 1	13.89%
6	Total of 6	4.63%	17 to 1	16.67%
7	Total of 7	6.94%	12 to 1	9.72%
8	Total of 8	9.72%	8 to 1	12.50%
9	Total of 9	11.57%	6 to 1	18.98%
10	Total of 10	12.50%	6 to 1	12.50%
11	Total of 11	12.50%	6 to 1	12.50%
12	Total of 12	11.57%	6 to 1	18.98%
13	Total of 13	9.72%	8 to 1	12.50%
14	Total of 14	6.94%	12 to 1	9.72%
15	Total of 15	4.63%	17 to 1	16.67%
16	Total of 16	2.78%	30 to 1	13.89%
17	Total of 17	1.39%	60 to 1	15.28%
One-of-a-kind	Specific number from 1 to 6	1 match: 34.72% 2 matches: 6.94% 3 matches: 0.46%	1 match: 1 to 1 2 matches: 2 to 1 3 matches: 3 to 1	7.87%
Two-of-a-kind	Specified two-dice combination[1]	13.89%	5 to 1	16.67%
Double	Specified pair[2]	7.41%	10 to 1	18.52%
Triple	Specified trips[3]	0.46%	180 to 1	16.20%
Any Triple	Any 3-of-a-kind	2.78%	30 to 1	13.89%

[1] Two-of-a-kind: Player may bet on any of the 15 possible two-dice combinations (e.g., 1, 2). The bet wins if both numbers appear.

[2] Double: Player may bet on any specific pair (e.g., two 1s). Player wins if at least two of the chosen numbers appear.

[3] Triple: Player may bet on any specific trips (e.g., three 1s). Player wins if all three dice match the number chosen.

A Grand Payout

The Grand Casino in Biloxi introduced Sic Bo with a mistake on the table layout. Instead of paying 60-1, bets on the 4 and 17 paid 80-1, resulting in a player edge of 12.5%. Gambling expert Stanford Wong got wind of this and posted the information on his Web site (www.bj21.com). Many of Wong's readers reacted quickly and flew to Biloxi to take advantage of the opportunity. The game lasted only a day after the pros hit it.

Summary

If you want to play, stick to the small and big bets only, where the edge is a reasonable 2.78%.

14

Slot Machines

Although slot machines provide the easiest way to play in a casino, they are the least understood of all the gambling options. In most other games, the odds are quantifiable, which means that the rules are disclosed, and by applying some math the odds can be determined. But, aside from specified minimums set by law, the player has almost no idea what he's up against when playing the "bandits." Minimum-return percentages are set at 75% in Nevada and 83% in Atlantic City, but in my opinion, there should be more available information. The player should have the right to know the odds of any game. Alas, I don't make the laws. But this chapter and Appendix E attempt to shed some new light on the topic of slot machines based on my research.

Return Percentages

In all machine games (slots, video poker, video keno) the value of a bet is expressed as a return percentage, as opposed to a house edge. To get from one to another, you must understand that the house edge plus the expected return always equals 100%. For example, if the expected return is 95% then the house edg is 5%.

Gaming-regulation entities in various jurisdictions disclose return percentages for "slots" on a monthly basis. The problem is, these statistics include all gaming *machines,* including video poker and video keno, which skew these reported numbers. I don't know of a source that separates reel slots from the other electronic games. For example, *Casino Player* magazine publishes combined slot statistics on a monthly basis, which is a good way to compare one casino region against another. However, video poker generally pays back more than reel slots, so the mix has the effect of raising the overall return. Normal fluctuation can also affect the results of such reports, which are based on actual, not theoretical, results. This is why casinos sometimes report more than a 100% return for the higher-denomination games.

In early 2004, in an effort to get at the theoretical return for just the reel slots, I contacted a casino executive in Laughlin, Nevada. His answers are shown in Table 35.

TABLE 35—Sample Slot Returns by Denomination

Denomination	Return Percentage
5¢	90%-92%
25¢	92%-93%
$1	94.5%-95.5%
$5	about 96%
$25	about 97%

"Participation slots" are slots that fall under a revenue-sharing agreement between the casino and the slot manufacturer. An 80/20 split is typical, with 80% going to the casino. According to sources in the business, participation slots are generally set to a return 88%-90%, which is low compared to other slots. A good, but not perfect, indicator of a particiaption slot is the presence of both a theme (built around a well-known television show, movie, or product) and a large progressive jackpot.

Be wary of advertising promising a particular return, say, 97.4%, for a group of slots (usually a bank, but sometimes an entire casino). Such claims will often be accompanied by small print with the key words "up to" being used, meaning that only one machine in the group is required to comply. And, of course, the playerwill have no idea which one.

In 2002, I devised a method (detailed on my Web site) for pinpointing the return percentages for nickel video slot machines. It was a rare instance of being able to make an apples-to-apples comparison of slot-machine returns. After conducting an exhaustive comparison, I posted the results and they were eventually published in the *Las Vegas Advisor*. The disclosure of this information created quite a stir in the industry. You can see the complete results of the survey in Appendix E.

How They Work

The father of modern slot machines is Inge S. Telnaes, who patented the concept that governs the way physical (as opposed to video) slot machines work. The basic concept of the Telnaes patent is that each stop on a slot machine reel is theoretically weighted. These weights are directly proportional to the probability that the reel will stop on that symbol. For example, the jackpot symbol may have a weight of 1, while the blanks above and below it have weights of 5 each. Thus, for every one time the reels stop on the jackpot symbol, they will stop one position away 10 times, on average.

Slot machines use a random number generator (RNG) to determine where the reels will stop. The machines are continuously drawing random numbers—thousands of them every second. The moment a player hits the button to spin the reels, one random number for each reel is chosen. Once the random numbers are chosen, they're mapped on a "virtual reel" to corresponding stops on the actual reels according to each stop's weight. The player's outcome is thus sealed the moment he hits the spin button.

Based on a study I conducted of a Double Strike slot machine in Reno in November 2000, I offer the following conclusions on how that machine was programmed to affect not only its ultimate return percentage, but also the way it performs.

The higher a symbol paid, the less it was weighted. The blanks above and below the highest paying symbols were weighted disproportionately high, resulting in a frequent near-miss effect. The first reel was weighted the most generously and the last reel the least, which creates more suspense. So while the machine may have been programmed to return about 94%, a high frequency of near misses may have given players a false sense that the odds were better than that. Again, this analysis was for a single machine, but it would seem logical that other slots are programmed in a similar manner.

Five-reel, multi-line, video-display slots do not use weighted reels. Rather, each stop is equally weighted. This is because the reels on videos are not limited like physical reels and may have as many stops as desired.

Variable-State Slots

Some slot machines have a feature in which the amount of a bonus payoff increases as the machine is played, with the bonus being won when it reaches a certain level or when a reel lands on the bonus symbol. Examples of this kind of machine include Piggy Bankin', Car Race, Temperature Rising, and Double Diamond Mine. It's possible to obtain an advantage by playing machines that were abandoned by a previous player with the bonus at a high level, but this secret has been out for a while and competition among "slot vultures" can be intense. Plus, the numbers of these machines have dwindled over the years, making them harder to come across in any state, let alone in a positive-return situation.

Slot Machine Myths and Facts

Of all the gambling games, more myths are attached to slot machines than anything else. Here are some of the most common, along with the facts of the matter.

Myth: Slot machines are programmed to go through a cycle of payoffs. Although the cycle can span thousands of spins, once it reaches the end, the outcomes will repeat themselves in exactly the same order as the last cycle.

Fact: There are no predetermined or predictable cycles. Every trial is random and independent of past trials.

Myth: Slot machines are programmed to pay off a set percentage of money bet. Thus, after a jackpot is hit, the machine will tighten up to get back into balance. Conversely, when a jackpot has not been hit for a long time, it's overdue and more likely to hit.

Fact: Again, each spin is random and independent. The odds are always the same as they were on the last spin. The only exception that I know of are "fruit machines" in England, which are guaranteed to pay back a minimum return in the short run.

Myth: Hot/cold coins are more likely to yield good returns.

Fact: The temperature of coins does not matter.

Myth: Using a slot card will cause machines to pay less.

Fact: Not true. The mechanism that determines where the reels stop does not know whether or not a player card is being used.

Myth: The loosest slot machines are placed [insert your favorite location here].

Fact: My research has found this to be untrue. Most casinos have a consistent slot-return policy across a given denomination. Those that do mix up loose and tight machines seem to do so randomly.

Myth: The casinos have a switch that lets them tighten all their slots on a busy weekend.

Fact: Again, not true. To change the return of a machine, someone has to open each machine individually and change what is called an EPROM (Erasable Programmable Read Only Memory) chip, which determines the reel weightings, and thus, the theoretical return. Paperwork disclosing the change must also be filed with gaming regulators. In short, it's too much work for a short-term change.

Summary

There isn't much to say about strategy in a game where you simply push a button. However, choosing which machine to play is still important. Using whatever resources you have to pick a casino with loose slots will help (e.g., payback charts in industry magazines). Sometimes casinos promise a specified return on all machines in a grouping; for example, a dollar carousel may indicate that machines are set to pay back *at least* 97.4%, which is a competitive return.

Many gambling writers advise players to always play maximum coins. The reason, they argue, is that jackpots usually pay more per coin based on a max-coin bet. While this is true, I disagree with the advice. I believe that given the choice of playing max coins on a lower denomination or one coin on a higher denomination, the later option is preferable. That is, the increase in return rate for higher-denomination machines usually outweighs the max-coin incentive on the lower denomination. So, if you normally play max coins on a 25¢ machine, I encourage you to instead play one coin on a 50¢ or $1 machine. Machines that are obviously jackpot heavy, e.g., progressives, are exceptions.

15

Sports Betting NFL

Sports betting is a never-ending topic about which numerous books have been written. This chapter only scratches the surface by covering various betting options in the NFL. Unlike most gambling games, the house edge in sports betting isn't always clear cut. That's because while your skill in wagering will affect the edge, it's usually impossible to quantify skill level perfectly. My philosophy in sports betting is to avoid handicapping completely and base decisions on historical experience of similar games. The information in this chapter is based on every NFL game from the 1983 season to the 2003 season, except Super Bowls. I exclude Super Bowls, because many tables are cut by home-field advantage and the Super Bowl is generally played on a neutral field.

A word of caution. There are only 266 games in a season, which creates an insufficient sample-size problem in analyzing NFL bets. Use the tables in this chapter with a grain of salt.

Pointspread Bets

In preparation for this chapter, I asked numerous people and sports book ticket writers what a bet using the pointspread is called. I have yet to receive a straight answer. Most claim that it's called a "straight bet," but this term can also be used to describe any bet on just one game (as opposed to a parlay or teaser, for example). So for lack of a better term, I'll call a bet against the pointspread a "pointspread bet."

Most casinos use a "20¢ line" (also called a line with "10¢ juice") for pointspread bets. This means the bettor must lay $1.10 to win $1.00. This type of line is most commonly used for betting football and basketball. Ignoring ties, the house edge on straight bets is 4.55% for a bettor picking teams randomly. However, about 2.63% of pointspread bets end in a tie, which lowers the house edge to 4.43%. A pointspread with a 10¢ line or "5¢ juice" describes the case where the bettor has to lay only $1.05 to win $1. Sometimes casinos offer 5¢ juice during promotions, the equivalent of a betting happy hour. This lowers the house edge to 2.32% counting ties.

For bettors who have no opinion on the probable outcome of a game and simply wish to bet with as little effort as possible, two pieces of information are pertinent in every bet: the home-field advantage and favored-team advantage.

In the 21-year sample period, home teams won 58.75% of the time. Home teams also outscored away teams by 3.03 points on average. As a rule of thumb, oddsmakers consider home-field advantage to be worth three points, which is just about right. Table 36 shows the results against the spread for both home and away teams. The last row shows that home teams have covered the spread 50.22% of the games not ending exactly on the pointspread. The extra 0.22% could easily be due to sample variation.

Not surprisingly, the favorite usually wins. In the sample period, the favorite won the game outright 66.26% of the time. However, against the spread the underdog has historically been the better bet. Table 37 on page 86 shows that the underdog covered the spread 51.81% of the time, not counting games where the outcome fell exactly on the number. With a 51.81% probability of winning against 10¢ juice, the house edge is 1.07%. Against 5¢ juice, the odds flip to the player's side with a player edge of 1.12%.

TABLE 36—Home vs. Away Outcomes Against Spread

Season	Home Win	Away Win	Tie	Prob. Home Win*	Prob. Away Win*
1983	105	119	8	46.88%	53.13%
1984	105	124	3	45.85%	54.15%
1985	128	100	4	56.14%	43.86%
1986	109	118	5	48.02%	51.98%
1987	100	115	3	46.51%	53.49%
1988	112	117	3	48.91%	51.09%
1989	109	118	5	48.02%	51.98%
1990	123	106	5	53.71%	46.29%
1991	121	107	6	53.07%	46.93%
1992	116	115	3	50.22%	49.78%
1993	109	118	7	48.02%	51.98%
1994	107	119	8	47.35%	52.65%
1995	122	122	6	50.00%	50.00%
1996	139	109	2	56.05%	43.95%
1997	110	125	15	46.81%	53.19%
1998	134	105	11	56.07%	43.93%
1999	128	123	7	51.00%	49.00%
2000	120	132	6	47.62%	52.38%
2001	124	119	15	51.03%	48.97%
2002	134	128	4	51.15%	48.85%
2003	132	126	8	51.16%	48.84%
Total	**2487**	**2465**	**134**	**50.22%**	**49.78%**

*Not counting ties

Tables 36 and 37 show that home teams are marginally superior bets to visiting teams and underdogs are significantly better than favorites. Combining the two, betting only on home underdogs, the historical outcome is even better. Table 38 on page 87 shows how well home underdogs have done over the sample period. If the bettor bet all games over the sample period against 10¢ juice, he would have shown a 1.46% profit. Against 5¢ juice the profit would have been 3.53%.

TABLE 37—Favorite vs. Dog
Outcomes Against the Spread

Season	Favorite Win	Dog Win	Tie	Prob. Favorite Win*	Prob. Dog Win*
1983	102	119	8	46.15%	53.85%
1984	111	116	3	48.90%	51.10%
1985	117	105	4	52.70%	47.30%
1986	105	120	5	46.67%	53.33%
1987	93	118	3	44.08%	55.92%
1988	109	114	3	48.88%	51.12%
1989	106	117	5	47.53%	52.47%
1990	121	102	5	54.26%	45.74%
1991	114	112	6	50.44%	49.56%
1992	110	116	3	48.67%	51.33%
1993	102	123	7	45.33%	54.67%
1994	102	118	8	46.36%	53.64%
1995	113	126	6	47.28%	52.72%
1996	120	122	2	49.59%	50.41%
1997	105	123	15	46.05%	53.95%
1998	127	110	11	53.59%	46.41%
1999	114	137	7	45.42%	54.58%
2000	116	133	6	46.59%	53.41%
2001	115	123	15	48.32%	51.68%
2002	118	142	4	45.38%	54.62%
2003	127	127	8	50.00%	50.00%
Total	**2347**	**2523**	**134**	**48.19%**	**51.81%**

* Not counting ties

Money Lines

Money lines are bets on who will win a game outright. Since there is no pointspread to level the playing field, to bet the favorite you must risk more than you'll win. For example, a money line of -150 means the player must risk $150 to win $100, or any proportion therein. A bettor on the underdog is rewarded with better than even money if his team wins (ex

TABLE 38—Home Dogs vs. Visiting Favorite Outcomes Against the Spread

Season	Home Dog Win	Visiting Favorite Win	Tie	Prob. Home Win*	Prob. Away Win*
1983	33	31	1	51.56%	48.44%
1984	35	42	2	45.45%	54.55%
1985	42	35	2	54.55%	45.45%
1986	38	36	2	51.35%	48.65%
1987	38	32	0	54.29%	45.71%
1988	30	29	1	50.85%	49.15%
1989	35	35	1	50.00%	50.00%
1990	32	32	3	50.00%	50.00%
1991	42	35	5	54.55%	45.45%
1992	44	39	0	53.01%	46.99%
1993	37	32	4	53.62%	46.38%
1994	30	28	4	51.72%	48.28%
1995	41	37	1	52.56%	47.44%
1996	40	25	0	61.54%	38.46%
1997	35	33	3	51.47%	48.53%
1998	39	33	3	54.17%	45.83%
1999	54	40	4	57.45%	42.55%
2000	39	37	1	51.32%	48.68%
2001	41	35	6	53.95%	46.05%
2002	51	36	1	58.62%	41.38%
2003	37	34	4	52.11%	47.89%
Total	**813**	**716**	**48**	**53.17%**	**46.83%**

* Not counting ties

cept you may still have to lay odds on a small underdog). For example, a money line of +130 means the bettor will win $130 for a $100 bet, or again any proportion therein.

The house edge in money line bets depends on how far apart the casino sets the two lines on the same game. The closer the lines, the less the house advantage. About the best the player can expect is a 10¢ or "dime" line, meaning the two money lines are 10 points apart, as in +150 and -160. Although 10¢ and 15¢ lines are seen in baseball, 20¢ lines are the norm in football. Regardless of the sports book policy, the money lines always get farther apart as games get more lopsided. For example, if the favored team had an 80% chance of winning the sports book might set the money lines at +300 and -500.

TABLE 39—Probability of Winning by Pointspread/Money Lines

Line	Favorite Wins	Dog Wins	Tie	Prob. Favorite Wins	Estimated Probability	Fair Money Line
-1	101	92	1	52.33%	47.02%	-/+ 113
-1.5	108	104	0	50.94%	49.91%	+/- 100
-2	86	120	0	41.75%	52.66%	+/- 111
-2.5	189	146	1	56.42%	55.27%	+/- 124
-3	418	261	2	61.56%	57.74%	+/- 137
-3.5	248	163	0	60.34%	60.07%	+/- 150
-4	180	96	0	65.22%	62.26%	+/- 165
-4.5	114	72	0	61.29%	64.31%	+/- 180
-5	111	57	3	66.07%	66.22%	+/- 196
-5.5	143	58	1	71.14%	67.99%	+/- 212
-6	166	68	0	70.94%	69.62%	+/- 229
-6.5	171	84	0	67.06%	71.11%	+/- 246
-7	290	100	1	74.36%	72.46%	+/- 263
-7.5	109	49	0	68.99%	73.67%	+/- 280
-8	98	34	0	74.24%	74.74%	+/- 296
-8.5	80	18	0	81.63%	75.67%	+/- 311
-9	84	22	0	79.25%	76.46%	+/- 325
-9.5	89	25	0	78.07%	77.11%	+/- 337
-10	100	24	1	80.65%	77.62%	+/- 347
-10.5	74	19	0	79.57%	77.99%	+/- 354
-11	51	17	0	75.00%	78.22%	+/- 359
-11.5	30	5	0	85.71%	78.31%	+/- 361
-12	36	3	0	92.31%	78.26%	+/- 360
-12.5	21	7	0	75.00%	78.07%	+/- 356
-13	28	10	0	73.68%	77.74%	+/- 349
-13.5	44	13	0	77.19%	77.27%	+/- 340
-14	42	9	0	82.35%	76.66%	+/- 328

Unfortunately my NFL database does not contain money lines. However, we can estimate the probability of winning based on the pointspread. Table 39 shows the historical outcomes for spreads of 1 to 14. The "Estimated Probability" column smooths out the ups and down and the "Fair Money Line" column shows a fair set of money lines based on the estimated probabilities. Due to a small sample size, this table should be considered to be only a rough guide.

Table 40 shows the actual probabilities and estimated probabilities from Table 39. The low actual probability of 2-point favorites drags down the estimated probabilities on small favorites. The high actual probability of winning for 12-point favorites causes the estimated probability to taper off after 12. It should be noted that both of these are obviously unrealistic assumptions.

TABLE 40—Probability of Winning by Pointspread

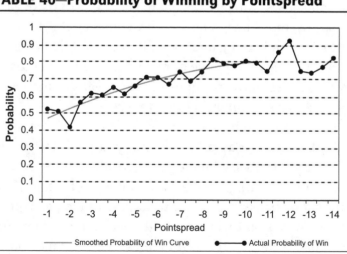

In 2004 I did a comparative study among both Las Vegas and off-shore sports books on money lines in the NFL. The most competitive money lines off-shore were at Pinnacle (pinnaclesports.com). Nobody else even came close. Pinnacle offers 10¢ money-line spreads in the NFL up to lines of +175 and -185 on the same game. All others start at 20¢ spreads. Among Las Vegas casinos, most games had 20¢ money lines at all casinos. However, on lopsided games I found the Golden Nugget to have the smallest spread between lines (by the time you read this, that may no longer be the case, since the Golden Nugget is being sold). The Cal-Neva sports book, which can be found at the Tuscany (and a non-casino location in Henderson), came in second. More information on this study can be found on my Web site.

Parlays

A parlay is a way to bet on multiple sporting events to get a big payoff if all of them win. All picks are subject to the pointspread (though money lines can also be parlayed). If just one game loses, you lose the entire bet. If one or more games are a draw, those are ignored. Parlay winners get paid according to the number of games won. In the event that all games bet result in ties except one or none, the entire bet becomes a push. Table 41 shows the house edge for various numbers of picks and pays assuming a random picker.

Parlay bets can be made either "off the board" or "on the card." To bet a parlay off the board, you go to the window and state your picks, with the pointspread on the board being used. To bet a parlay on the card, you fill out a card (found in the sports books) with your picks against the pointspreads that are stated on the card. For the recreational gambler, if you must make a 2- or 3-team parlay bet, I recommend betting off the board. If you must make a 4-team or more parlay, parlay cards usually offer higher payouts. Also, parlay cards can be exploited to a degree by picking games in which the line on the board has moved in your favor relative to the card, especially onto or off of the critical 3- and 7-point margins of victory in football.

TABLE 41—Parlay Edge by Number of Teams/Payout

Teams	Pays	House Edge
2	2.5	12.50%
2	2.6*	10.00%
2	2.7	7.50%
2	2.8	5.00%
2	2.9	2.50%
3	5	25.00%
3	6*	12.50%
4	10*	31.25%
4	11	25.00%
4	12	18.75%
4	13	12.50%
4	14	6.25%
5	20	34.00%
5	25	18.75%
5	30	3.13%
6	30	51.56%
6	35	43.75%
6	40	35.94%
6	45	28.13%
6	50	20.31%
6	55	12.50%
6	60	4.69%
20	200,000	80.93%

*Standard Las Vegas pricing.

Following are the formulas for the parlay card house edge according to the number of teams played.

	Off the Board	Card
• 3-teamer	7-payout)/8	(8-payout)/8
• 4-teamer	(15-payout)/16	(16-payout)/16
• 5-teamer	(31-payout)/32	(32-payout)/32
• 6-teamer	(63-payout)/64	(64-payout)/64
• 7-teamer	(127-payout)/128	(128-payout)/128
• 8-teamer	(255-payout)/256	(256-payout)/256
• 9-teamer	(511-payout)/512	(512-payout)/512
• 10-teamer	(1023-payout)/1024	(1024-payout)/1024

Note that parlay-card payoffs are all "for 1," so a 3-team parlay with a win of 7 for 1 is equivalent to a 3-team off-the-board parlay paying 6 "to 1" (6-1). Here are some examples. The Golden Nugget pays 52 *for* 1 on a 6-team parlay card, for a house edge of (64-52)/64 = 18.75%. Coast casinos pay 40 *to* 1 on a 6-team off-the-board parlay, for a house edge of (63-40)/64 = 35.94%.

In 2004, the Golden Nugget in Las Vegas offered a "$1,000,000 Parlay Card," which paid a million dollars for a $5 bet, or 200,000-1 payoff odds. For a 50% picker, this card carried an 80.93% house edge (ouch!), before even considering that ties lose.

Teasers

Teasers are offered in football and basketball, but NFL sides offer the best opportunity to profit from them. A teaser is similar to a parlay, except you're given a line movement of 6, 6.5, or 7 points in your favor on all picks (e.g., if the line is +1, you get +7 on a 6-point teaser). Of course, nothing is free—the payoff odds for a teaser are much less than for a parlay. I'll focus here on the 6-point teaser, which offers the best odds.

Over the sample period of my data, the probability of victory with a free 6 points on both sides of all games is 68.67%, not counting ties. Unfortunately, to have a breakeven chance

TABLE 42—House Edge for Random Teasers (Coast)

Teams	Prob. Win	Pays	House Edge
2	47.15%	10 to 11	9.98%
3	32.38%	9 to 5	9.33%
4	22.24%	3 to 1	11.06%
5	15.27%	9 to 2	16.02%
6	10.49%	7 to 1	16.12%

on a 2-team 6-point teaser paying 10-11, the probability of winning each game must be 72.37%. And the percentage tends to get even higher when you tease more than two teams. Table 42 shows the probability of winning and the house edge for the Las Vegas Coast Casinos teasers, which are the most generous that I know of.

An understanding of the margin-of-victory distribution is critical to improving your teaser odds. Table 43 on page 94 shows the frequency and probability of each margin of victory over the sample period.

Note that 23.42% of games fall on a margin of victory of 3 or 7 and 37.91% fall between, or include, 3 to 7. In his book *Sharp Sports Betting*, Stanford Wong advises teasing across the 3- and 7-point margin of victories. Professional bettor Fezzik has long recommended these teasers, labeling them "no-brainers." (Additionally, he recommends that only home teams be teased, as this subset has historically been the most profitable.) For example, teasing a 2-point underdog to +8 points results in covering the game spread even if that team loses by 3 or 7 points. Pointspreads that cross over both the 3- and 7-point margin of victories on a teaser are +1.5 to +2.5 (teasing up) and -7.5 to -8.5 (teasing down). Over the sample period, teasing just these games results in a probability of winning per game of 73.52%. Table 44 on page 95 shows the player advantage and the probability of winning these "Wong teasers" at Coast Casinos' payoff odds.

Although the odds get better as the number of teams on the teaser goes up, on any given week there usually aren't many games that qualify for a Wong teaser. On average, only 21.77% of games qualify. So in a 16-game week, on average, there will be only 3.48 good games to tease. When you find a good week with lots of opportunities but are uncomfortable putting everything on one bet, you might consider crafting a 3- or 4-team round robin, in which you cover every subset from among the good games.

TABLE 43—Probability of Margin of Victory

Margin of Victory	Number	Probability
0	10	0.20%
1	217	4.27%
2	190	3.74%
3	782	15.38%
4	284	5.58%
5	160	3.15%
6	293	5.76%
7	409	8.04%
8	130	2.56%
9	93	1.83%
10	295	5.80%
11	167	3.28%
12	83	1.63%
13	159	3.13%
14	237	4.66%
15	83	1.63%
16	113	2.22%
17	196	3.85%
18	107	2.10%
19	60	1.18%
20	133	2.62%
21	133	2.62%
22	42	0.83%
23	61	1.20%
24	108	2.12%
25	47	0.92%
26	33	0.65%
27	85	1.67%
28	76	1.49%
29 or more	300	5.90%
Total	**5086**	**1**

TABLE 44—Probability of Winning Wong Teasers (Coast)

Teams	Prob. Win	Pays	Player Advantage
2	54.05%	10 to 11	3.19%
3	39.74%	9 to 5	11.28%
4	29.22%	3 to 1	16.87%
5	21.48%	9 to 2	18.15%
6	15.79%	7 to 1	26.35%

Breaking down the Wong teasers even further I show the following, based on all games from 1983 through 2004:

Teasers	Prob. of Win
Home underdogs of 1.5 to 2.5 points	75.52%
Visiting underdogs of 1.5 to 2.5 points	71.53%
Home favorites of 7.5 to 8.5 points	70.30%
Visiting favorites of 7.5 to 8.5 points	67.31%

Fezzik agreed that the first- and last-place positions were roughly correct, but feels that the second and third positions should be reversed, believing that my ordering reflects a small sample size. He recommends teasing only the home teams.

The Best Odds

There are lots of factors that go into the overall rating of a sports book. Among them, the juice on pointspread bets, the spreads on money-line bets, the payoffs on parlays, the maximum amounts you can bet, cashback, the variety of betting options, and overall ambiance.

Most bets made are against a pointspread, so I believe this consideration merits special attention. In almost all cases, the bettor must lay 10¢ juice (bet $11 to win $10), but some sports books have exceptions on the NFL. In the most recent NFL season, specials offering 5¢ juice (bet $10.50 to win $10) were available during promotional periods or for the Super Bowl at the following Las Vegas casinos: Hilton, El Cortez, Arizona Charlie's (Decatur and Boulder), Stratosphere, Park Place casinos, Coast casinos, and Station casinos.

Cashback (slot club-style rebates on your wagers) should also be factored into deciding where to bet. Following are cashback rates that I am aware of: Circus Circus: .8%, Imperial Palace: .8%, Hilton: .8%, Park Place casinos: .25%, and Coast casinos: 0.2%

Touts

In general, I'm skeptical about touts, meaning handicappers who charge for their picks. It's virtually impossible to distinguish the good touts from the bad without consulting an independent third party. Touts claiming a long-term success rate of over 60% should be avoided, as it's virtually impossible to achieve this kind of accuracy over the long run. Also avoid services with multiple levels of clubs; such as gold, silver, and bronze. Two sources I do trust are sharpsportsbetting.com and lvasports.com, which offer honestly documented track records of their touts.

Summary

Winning at sports betting is very difficult. Unless you know what you're doing, I recommend that you avoid exotic bets (parlays and teasers) and stick with the basic bets (pointspreads, totals, and money lines). Regardless of the sport or type of bet, shop around for the best lines. Be wary of touts. A good indicator of a legitimate tout is one who offers proof of his success rate without a multi-level scheme. To have the best chance with the minimum amount of work on NFL bets, simply bet home underdogs against the pointspread.

16

Texas Hold 'Em Poker

Poker is often called the king of gambling games, and I agree. It's the perfect microcosm of life, requiring sharp analytical skills as well as the ability to outwit your opponents. There are numerous books about poker that cover the game's many complexities. It's difficult to provide relevant material in a short chapter about a game players could spend a whole life studying. However, the information in the tables that follow should provide value for a beginning study of Texas hold 'em.

Starting Cards

Choosing which initial 2-card hands to play is a decision you face every hand in poker. Beginners tend to want to see a flop with almost every 2-card hand. This is a big mistake. Your probability of winning is highly correlated to the strength of your hole cards. The best starting hands are the highest pairs (Aces, Kings, Queens, and Jacks) and suited high cards (AK, AQ, KQ, etc.). One of the most popular areas of my Web site ranks the starting hands according to the number of players. The rankings for a 10-player game that appears in Appendix F will give you a gauge by which to value starting hands.

My Web site has similar tables for 2-, 3-, 4-, 6-, and 8-player games. As the number of players goes down, the value of pairs and high cards goes up, while suited and connected cards goes down.

Many introductory poker books cover starting hands in much greater depth.

Pot Odds

In hold 'em, you'll often find yourself in a position where you are one card away from a flush or straight. The best way to play the hand depends on lots of things, including the probability of making the hand, the amount you will win if you do, and the amount of the bet when it's your turn to act. Table 45 on the next page shows three common hands after the flop (the point where there are two cards left to deal), the probability of making the hand, and the pot odds. You calculate pot odds in poker to determine if it's profitable to continue in a hand. To figure the pot odds, divide the amount in the pot by how much it costs to call. For example, if there's $50 in the pot, and you have to call $10 to continue, then the pot is offering you 5 to 1 pot odds not to fold. If your hand has greater than a 1-in-5 chance of winning, then it's mathematically profitable to call.

The most common drawing hands where pot odds come into play are draws to straights and flushes. The numbers in Table 45 assume that you always win when you make a hand, and include no consideration of money bet at later betting stages in the hand. Many factors come into the play of a given hand, but pot odds are the best starting point from which to make your decisions.

Let's look at an example. Suppose you have the ace of clubs and any other club. The flop has two clubs, so you have four to the nut flush (the best possible flush). If there's $20 in the pot and the bet is $5 to you, should you call? In this case, the ratio of pot to bet is 4, which is much greater than the 1.86 required. So the pot odds tell you that calling is profitable.

TABLE 45—Pot Odds After the Flop

Hand	Probability of Making Hand	Pot Odds
4 to a flush	34.97%	1.86
4 to an open-end straight	31.45%	2.18
4 to an inside straight	16.47%	5.07

Table 46 shows the same figures but after the turn (when there is only one card left to come). Obviously, in this spot the pot needs to be much larger to warrant staying in.

TABLE 46—Pot Odds After the Turn

Pot Odds—After Turn

Hand	Probability of Making Hand	Pot Odds
4 to a flush	19.57%	4.11
4 to an open-end straight	17.39%	4.75
4 to an inside straight	8.70%	10.50

Summary

Obviously, this chapter only scratches the surface of a very complex game. My goal was to introduce two important topics. Appendix H contains suggestions for further reading.

17

Three Card Poker

Three Card Poker is one of the most successful new table games. Over the years, different paytables have come along, which makes it important to be able to distinguish good schedules from bad.

Pair Plus

The pair plus bet pays based on the player's hand only, thus no skill is required and it can be analyzed easily.

Table 47 shows how often the player will be dealt each hand in Three Card Poker. Note that the order of hands is not the same as in standard five-card poker. In particular, a straight is less likely, and thus ranked higher, than a flush.

TABLE 47—Probabilities in Three Card Poker

Hand	Combinations	Probability
Straight flush	48	0.0021719
3-of-a-kind	52	0.0023529
Straight	720	0.0325792
Flush	1096	0.0495928
Pair	3744	0.1694118
Queen to ace high	9720	0.4398190
Jack high or less	6720	0.3040724
Total	**22100**	**1**

Table 48 shows some of the paytables I've seen for the pair plus bet.

TABLE 48—Three Card Poker Pair Plus Paytables

Hand	Schedules					
	A	B	C	D	E	F
Straight flush	40-1	40-1	35-1	50-1	40-1	40-1
3-of-a-kind	30-1	25-1	25-1	30-1	30-1	30-1
Straight	6-1	6-1	6-1	6-1	5-1	6-1
Flush	4-1	4-1	4-1	3-1	4-1	3-1
Pair	1-1	1-1	1-1	1-1	1-1	1-1
House edge	2.32%	3.49%	4.58%	5.10%	5.57%	7.28%

Unfortunately the norm, in Las Vegas at least, is paytable F, with a house edge of 7.28%. If you remember just one thing from this chart, it should be that if the flush pays only 3, you should avoid the Pair Plus bet.

Ante

There are also different paytables for the bonus on the ante bet, as shown in Table 49. Fortunately, most casinos use schedule A, which has the lowest house edge at 3.37%.

TABLE 49—Three Card Poker Ante Bonus

Hand	Schedules			
	A	B	C	D
Straight flush	5-1	5-1	4-1	3-1
3-of-a-kind	4-1	3-1	3-1	2-1
Straight	1-1	1-1	1-1	1-1
House edge	3.37%	3.61%	3.83%	4.28%

Strategy

Optimal strategy on the ante bet is to raise with a hand of Q64 or better. This is true for all bonus paytables.

Flashing Dealers

As first explained by James Grosjean in *Beyond Counting*, when Three Card Poker is dealt from a shuffling machine, which it usually is, the dealer sometimes flashes (shows) the bottom card as she takes her hand from the shuffler. This is not done intentionally, but seeing this card can yield a significant player advantage.

Following is the playing strategy taking into account the card the dealer exposes:

Jack or less: Always raise
Queen: Raise with Q92 or higher
King: Raise with K92 or higher
Ace: Raise with A92 or higher
Unknown face card: Raise with QJ5 or higher

The player advantage if you can always see a single dealer's card, assuming ante bonus schedule A, is 3.48%. If you can tell only that the card is or isn't a face card, the player advantage is 2.41%.

Summary

Like most new casino games, the house edge in Three Card Poker is higher than the classic gambling games, such as blackjack, baccarat, and craps. If you play, I advise betting in moderation and mainly for the entertainment factor rather than to win money. The two most important things to remember from this chapter are to raise on Q64 or higher and avoid the pair plus bet if the flush pays only 3.

18

Video Poker

Entire books have been written about video poker and even most of those only scratch the surface. There are lots of games, numerous paytables for each game, and different strategies for each paytable. It gets even more complicated when you factor in cashback, promotions, and trying to keep up to date with where the good games are. This chapter concentrates only on the return percentages of some old and new common games and paytables and the strategies for Jacks or Better and Deuces Wild.

Paytables

The odds on electronic games, such as video poker and slots, are measured by return percentage. Of course, most return percentages are less than 100%, which is how the casinos make money. However, in some video poker games, the return is over 100%, which means that a skilled player has the advantage. All return percentages listed here assume playing according to the optimal strategy. Although only the most expert players can do this, video poker strategy cards and software can produce near optimal, but much simpler, strategies for most games.

The most important decision in video poker is which game to play. The paytable is critical to your expected return, regardless of your skill level. Table 50 shows the expected return for various games and common paytables. Although the listed percentages are for play with the optimal strategy, the degree of difference in playing results will be roughly the same regardless of your level of playing skill.

Contrary to popular myth, the cards in video poker games are randomly and fairly dealt, as if in a live game. This is a strict law in Nevada, and the major U.S. slot makers adhere to it in all jurisdictions. However, anything is possible when third-rate manufacturers provide machines for small markets and foreign countries lacking proper regulation.

TABLE 50—Return Percentages for Common Video Poker Paytables

Jacks or Better

Royal flush	940	800	800	800	800	800	800	800	800
Straight flush	50	50	50	50	50	50	50	50	50
4-of-a-kind	25	25	80	25	80	25	80	25	25
Full house	9	9	8	9	8	8	7	7	6
Flush	6	6	6	5	5	5	5	5	5
Straight	4	4	4	4	4	4	4	4	4
3-of-a-kind	3	3	3	3	3	3	3	3	3
2 pair	2	2	1	2	1	2	1	2	2
Jacks/bet.	1	1	1	1	1	1	1	1	1
Return	**99.90%**	**99.54%**	**98.49%**	**98.45%**	**97.40%**	**97.30%**	**96.25%**	**96.15%**	**95.00%**

Bonus Poker

Royal flush	800	800	800
Straight flush	50	50	50
4 aces	80	80	80
4 2s, 3s or 4s	40	40	40
4 5-K	25	25	25
Full house	8	7	6
Flush	5	5	5
Straight	4	4	4
3-of-a-kind	3	3	3
Two pair	2	2	2
Jacks or better	1	1	1
Return	**99.17%**	**98.01%**	**96.87%**

Double Bonus Poker

Royal flush	800	800	800	800	800	800
Straight flush	50	50	50	50	50	50
4 aces	160	160	160	160	160	160
4 2s, 3s or 4s	80	80	80	80	80	80
4 5-K	50	50	50	50	50	50
Full house	10	9	9	9	9	9
Flush	7	7	6	6	7	6
Straight	5	5	5	4	4	4
3-of-a-kind	3	3	3	3	3	3
Two pair	1	1	1	1	1	1
Jacks or better	1	1	1	1	1	1
Return	**100.17%**	**99.11%**	**97.81%**	**96.49%**	**97.74%**	**96.38%**

Double Double Bonus Poker

Royal flush	800	800	800	800	800
Straight flush	50	50	50	50	50
4 aces w/ 2-4	400	400	400	400	400
4 2-4 w/ A-4	160	160	160	160	160
4 aces	160	160	160	160	160
4 2-4	80	80	80	80	80
4 5-K	50	50	50	50	50
Full house	10	9	9	8	6
Flush	6	6	5	5	5
Straight	4	4	4	4	4
3-of-a-kind	3	3	3	3	3
Two pair	1	1	1	1	1
Jacks/bet.	1	1	1	1	1
Return	**100.07%**	**98.98%**	**97.87%**	**96.79%**	**94.66%**

Double Double Aces & Faces

Royal flush	800	800	800	800	800	800	800	800
Straight flush	50	50	50	50	50	50	50	50
Four A + J-K	320	320	320	320	320	320	320	320
Four A + 2-10	160	160	160	160	160	160	160	160
Four J-K + J-A	160	160	160	160	160	160	160	160
Four J-K + 2-10	80	80	80	80	80	80	80	80
Four 2-10	50	50	50	50	50	50	50	50
Full house	12	8	9	9	10	8	9	8
Flush	5	7	6	7	6	7	6	5
Straight	4	5	5	4	4	4	4	4
3-of-a-kind	3	3	3	3	3	3	3	3
Two pair	1	1	1	1	1	1	1	1
Pair	1	1	1	1	1	1	1	1
Non-paying hand	0		0	0	0	0	0	0
Return	**101.14%**	**100.47%**	**100.35%**	**100.17%**	**100.03%**	**99.10%**	**98.94%**	**96.77%**

Deuces Wild

Natural royal	800	800	800	800	800	800	800	800	800
4 deuces	200	200	200	200	200	200	200	200	200
Wild royal	25	25	20	25	25	25	20	25	25
5-of-a-kind	15	16	12	15	16	16	10	15	15
Straight flush	9	10	9	9	13	13	8	10	9
4-of-a-kind	5	4	5	4	4	4	4	4	4
Full house	3	4	3	4	3	3	4	3	3
Flush	2	3	2	3	2	2	3	2	2
Straight	2	2	2	2	2	2	2	2	2
3-of-a-kind	1	1	1	1	1	1	1	1	1
Return	**100.76%**	**99.73%**	**98.94%**	**98.91%**	**96.73%**	**96.77%**	**95.96%**	**94.82%**	**94.34%**

Loose Deuces

Natural royal	800	800	800	800	800	800	800	800
4 deuces	500	500	500	500	500	500	500	500
Wild royal	25	25	25	25	25	25	25	25
5-of-a-kind	16	17	16	15	15	12	12	15
Straight flush	11	10	10	10	8	10	8	5
4-of-a-kind	4	4	4	4	4	4	4	4
Full house	3	3	3	3	3	3	3	3
Flush	2	2	2	2	2	2	2	2
Straight	2	2	2	2	2	2	2	2
3-of-a-kind	1	1	1	1	1	1	1	1
Return	**101.73%**	**101.60%**	**101.29%**	**100.97%**	**100.15%**	**100.02%**	**99.20%**	**99.07%**

Bonus Deuces Wild

Royal flush	800	800	800	800	800	800	800	800
4 deuces + ace	400	400	400	250	400	400	400	400
4 deuces + 2-K	200	200	200	200	200	200	200	200
5 aces	25	25	25	25	25	25	25	25
5 3-5	80	80	80	80	160	80	80	80
5 6-K	40	40	40	40	50	40	40	4
Wild royal flush	20	20	20	20	20	20	20	20
Straight flush	10	9	13	8	9	10	13	12
4-of-a-kind	4	4	4	4	4	4	4	4
Full house	4	4	3	4	3	3	3	3
Flush	3	3	3	3	2	3	2	2
Straight	1	1	1	1	1	1	1	1
3-of-a-kind	1	1	1	1	1	1	1	1
Return	**99.86%**	**99.45%**	**98.80%**	**98.65%**	**98.61%**	**97.36%**	**96.71%**	**96.22%**

Joker Poker

Royal flush	800	1000	800	800	800	800	940	800
5-of-a-kind	200	100	200	200	200	200	200	200
Wild royal	100	50	100	100	100	100	100	100
Straight flush	50	50	50	50	50	50	50	40
4-of-a-kind	20	20	20	17	15	20	15	20
Full house	7	8	6	7	8	6	7	5
Flush	5	7	5	5	5	4	5	4
Straight	3	5	3	3	3	3	3	3
3-of-a-kind	2	2	2	2	2	2	2	2
2 Pair	1	1	1	1	1	1	1	1
Kings/bet.	1	0	1	1	1	1	1	1
Return	**100.65%**	**99.08%**	**99.08%**	**98.09%**	**97.95%**	**97.58%**	**96.74%**	**95.46%**

Sequential Royal

Some video poker games pay a bonus (e.g., 10,000 coins with 5 coins bet) for a sequential royal flush. Unless otherwise stated on the machine, sequential royals pay one way only, from left to right. These games are rare, so I won't waste space with a lot of sequential-royal paytables. As a rule of thumb, if a paytable adds a win of 10,000 for a one-way sequential royal with 5 coins bet, it adds about 0.23% to the return. If the sequential royal pays in both directions, add 0.46% to the return.

New Games

At the time of this writing, the following video poker variants, One-Eyed Jacks, Five Aces, Shockwave, and Super Times Pay, are new and not widespread. Although there may be more popular games not covered in this book, I wanted to be among the first to write about these new additions to the video poker arena.

One-Eyed Jacks

In this game, the jacks of hearts and spades are optionally wild. I use the word "optionally," because if the player gets what would normally be a royal flush in hearts or spades, it still pays as a natural royal. There's previously been some confusion about how that hand is scored.

TABLE 51—Return Percentages for One-Eyed Jacks Paytables

Nat. Royal flush	800	800	800	800	800	800
Wild Royal flush	200	180	200	150	150	150
5-of-a-kind	75	80	75	75	75	75
Straight flush	50	50	45	50	45	40
4-of-a-kind	15	15	15	15	15	15
Full house	5	5	5	5	5	5
Flush	3	3	3	3	3	3
Straight	2	2	2	2	2	2
3-of-a-kind	1	1	1	1	1	1
Two pair	1	1	1	1	1	1
Return	**100.28%**	**99.98%**	**99.29%**	**98.96%**	**97.95%**	**96.97%**

Five Aces

The title just about says it all. There are five aces in the deck. The suit of the fifth ace is a star. Paytables I've seen are based on Double Double Bonus, Double Bonus, and Bonus Poker. Table 52 lumps all the games and paytables together.

TABLE 52—Return Percentages for Five Aces Paytables

Hand	Double Double Bonus			Double Bonus			Bonus Poker (Jacks or Better)		
Five Aces	1200	1200	1200	1200	1200	1200	1200	1200	1200
Royal flush	800	800	800	800	800	800	800	800	800
Straight flush	100	100	100	100	100	100	100	100	100
4 aces w/ 2-4	400	400	400	160	160	160	80	80	80
4 aces w/ 5-K	160	160	160	160	160	160	80	80	80
4 2-4 w/ A-4	160	160	160	80	80	80	40	40	40
4 2-4 w/ 5-K	80	80	80	80	80	80	40	40	40
4 5-K	50	50	50	50	50	50	25	25	25
Full house	8	7	6	8	8	7	9	9	7
Flush	5	5	5	6	5	5	6	5	5
Straight	4	4	4	4	4	4	4	4	4
3-of-a-kind	2	2	2	3	3	3	3	3	3
Two pair	1	1	1	1	1	1	1	1	1
Pair aces	1	1	1	1	1	1	1	1	1
Pair J-K	0	0	0	0	0	0	1	1	1
Return	**97.65%**	**96.61%**	**95.59%**	**99.02%**	**97.75%**	**96.65%**	**98.04%**	**97.05%**	**94.84%**

Note that Double Double Bonus and Double Bonus start paying at a pair of aces.

Shockwave

If you get a 4-of-a-kind, the game goes into "Shockwave" mode for the next 10 hands or until you hit another 4-of-a-kind, whichever happens first. In Shockwave mode, any 4-of-a-kind pays 800 per coin bet, the same as a royal flush. This calls for playing two different strategies, depending on whether you're in regular or Shockwave mode. Table 53 shows some paytables I've seen and the corresponding returns assuming optimal strategy.

TABLE 53—Return Percentages for Shockwave Paytables

Royal flush	800	800	800	800	800	800
Straight flush	100	100	100	100	100	100
4-of-a-kind–Shockwave mode	800	800	800	800	800	800
4-of-a-kind–Regular mode	25	25	25	25	25	25
Full house	12	11	10	10	9	9
Flush	8	8	8	7	6	6
Straight	5	5	5	5	5	4
3-of-a-kind	3	3	3	3	3	3
Two pair	1	1	1	1	1	1
Pair	1	1	1	1	1	1
Non-paying hand	0	0	0	0	0	0
Return	**99.55%**	**98.45%**	**97.34%**	**95.72%**	**93.23%**	**91.77%**

Super Times Pay

The player may bet 1 to 6 coins per game. For 1 to 5 coins, the game plays normally. For 6 coins bet, the paytable is the same as for 5 coins, but a multiplier feature kicks in. According to machines I've seen, every 15 hands the game multiplies the win by a random amount. The average of this random amount is 4.05.

On average, the sixth coin increase the overall win by 20.33%, for an additional 20% wagered, making the sixth coin marginally a good bet. The paytables used are common, thus the strategy is the same. For the return on a 6-coin bet, multiply the ordinary video poker return by 1.00278. The paytables I've seen had returns of 96.2%-97.1%.

Progressives

Machines with progressive meters for jackpots are available in most forms of video poker. Usually, instead of a fixed win for a royal flush, there's a progressive jackpot. Compared to fixed-paytable games, the lower hands pay a little less, but royal flushes average more. In my opinion, progressives are best left to the pros who know when the jackpots have gotten high enough to warrant playing. Using good video poker software or the probability tables found on my Web site, you can determine when a progressive is worth playing.

Also, be careful about playing multi-play video poker (Triple Play, Five Play, etc.). Given the same paytable, the odds per hand are the same as in single-line and can actually be a plus if you have a positive-return situation. However, as a general rule, the paytables are not as good on multi-play games. This is especially true of 50 Play and 100 Play games.

Strategy

The bad news is that optimal strategy in video poker is extremely complicated. The good news is that simplified strategies are available that are nearly as powerful and losses due to inaccuracy cost 0.1% or less.

Serious video poker players should have video poker strategy cards for the most common games or software that can produce the proper strategies for any game. There are several such products on the market (see Appendix H). Here I present simplified strategies for two popular games: Jacks or Better and Deuces Wild.

Unlike my advice for slot machines, in video poker you

should almost always play the maximum number of coins, due to the strong incentive on the royal flush payoff to play the full number of coins, which is usually five. Playing less than maximum coins reduces the return by about 1.4%. If betting max coins is too much for you, then drop to a lower denomination, but make sure the paytable is the same or better.

To use any of these strategies, look up all viable ways to play a hand and choose the option that's highest on the list. For example, with 2♣,2♥,5♣,8♣,J♣ in Jacks or Better, the three most viable plays are to keep the low pair, four to a flush, or the high card. The simple Jacks or Better strategy lists "4 to a flush" as the highest of the three viable plays, thus you should discard the 2♥ and hope to draw another club.

Jacks or Better Simple Strategy

If this strategy is played on a 9/6 Jacks or Better schedule, which pays 99.54% with optimal strategy, the return is 99.46% (so the cost due to inaccuracy of the strategy is only 0.08%).

full house or better
4 to a royal flush
straight, three of a kind, or flush
4 to a straight flush
2 pair
high pair (Jacks-Aces)
3 to a royal flush
4 to a flush
low pair
4 to an open-end straight (e.g., 6♠,7♥,8♦,9♦)
2 suited high cards
3 to a straight flush
2 unsuited high cards (if more than 2, pick lowest 2)
suited 10/J, 10/Q, or 10/K
one high card
discard everything

Deuces Wild Simple Strategy

In Deuces Wild, you never throw away a deuce; hence, the strategy on page 103 has been categorized according to the number of deuces. It was designed to be played against the full-pay paytable returning 100.76% with optimal strategy. Using the simplified strategy here will result in a return of 100.71%.

An intermediate strategy for Jacks or Better and optimal strategies for both Jacks or Better and Deuces Wild are listed in the video poker section of my Web site.

Summary

If you're a slot machine player, I highly recommend that you convert to video poker. It's more work, but the rewards are well worth it. It isn't difficult to get to a return of 99.5%, not including cashback and comps. With extra work, video poker is one of the few games where returns of over 100% are possible.

0 deuces

4 or 5 to a royal flush

any paying hand

4 to a straight flush

3 to a royal flush

pair

4 to a flush

4 to an open-end straight

3 to a straight flush

4 to an inside straight, except missing deuce (e.g., 4♠,6♦,7♥,8♣)

2 to a royal flush, J or Q high

1 deuce

any pat 4-of-a-kind or higher

4 to a royal flush

full house

4 to a straight flush with 3 consecutive singletons, 5-7 or higher

3-of-a-kind, straight, or flush

all other 4 to a straight flush

3 to a royal flush

3 to a straight flush with 2 consecutive singletons, 6-7 or higher

deuce only

2 deuces

any pat 4-of-a-kind or higher

4 to a royal flush

4 to a straight flush with 2 consecutive singletons, 6-7 or higher

2 deuces only

3 deuces

pat royal flush

3 deuces only

4 deuces

4 deuces

19

Frequently Asked Questions

Before this book was written, I answered questions for seven years from visitors to my Web site, wizardofodds.com. Here are some of the most frequently asked questions.

Q: What is your opinion about betting systems? Judging from what I read [in their advertising], they seem like an easy way to beat the casinos.

A: All betting systems that purport to beat negative-expectation games are equally worthless. Not only do betting systems fail to overcome the house advantage, but they can't even dent it. Computer simulations prove this every time. Millions have tried to beat the house with betting systems, yet the doors to the casinos are still wide open. Betting-system sellers are on the same level as pyramid and Ponzi scheme marketers—if their systems work so well, why wouldn't they just make millions themselves using them?

Q: I have a foolproof betting system that's going to make me richer than Bill Gates. You seem like a nice person and I'd like to share it with you if you can be sworn to secrecy.

A: No thanks; go ahead without me. You can write and say "I told you so" after you make your first million.

Q: I know you won't believe me, but I have a betting system that's so good it could bankrupt Vegas if the casinos don't stop me from using it. My question is, will the casinos bar me for winning too much?

A: No, they'll be happy to get your action. And in the event you get lucky and win big with a betting system, the major casinos will be happy to fly you back in a Lear jet in the hopes of winning it back, which they usually do. So go ahead, nothing is standing in your way—except the house edge.

Q: No, really, I have a betting system that will make me a multi-millionaire within one year. Remember my name, because by this time next year I'll be known as the man who killed Vegas.

A: I'll add it to my list of numerous other names that have made this claim.

Q: You say that if the ball lands on red 20 times in a row, the next spin is just as likely to be red as black. I disagree. The odds against 21 reds in a row must be staggering.

A: The odds against 21 reds on a fair wheel *are* staggering, but they're exactly the same as betting there will be 20 reds in a row and then one black. The roulette ball doesn't have a memory. The past does not matter in roulette and every spin is completely independent.

Q: As evidence that betting systems don't work, you cite that they can't beat a computer simulation. What good is that? Computers are worthless and unreliable in simulating casino games, because of factors like dealer signature in roulette. Furthermore, who makes a billion bets in real life? If it takes that long to kill my system, then that's okay with me. I won't live that long anyway.

A: Computer simulations are perfectly valid for testing real-world random events in any field of study. In fact, they're perfectly suited for modeling casino games, because the rules are so well quantifiable. I believe biases, such as dealer signature (a habit of always releasing the ball with the same speed), are strongly overrated and are of no practical help. Finally, remember that what can't be trusted over a billion bets also can't be trusted over one.

Q: I disagree that you should decline even money with a blackjack against a dealer ace. It's a sure winner!

A: In a 6-deck game, the probability the dealer will not have a blackjack in this situation is 69.26%. Assuming you made a $10 bet, the expected value of not taking even money on a blackjack is $15 x 69.26% = $10.39, 39¢ above the even-money option. Over the long run, that extra 39¢ will add up. Taking even money reduces your risk, but the objective should be to maximize your expectation. If you're afraid of losing, you probably shouldn't be gambling in the first place.

Q: Okay, you make a good mathematical argument that you should refuse even money. But you don't make a good psychological argument. The way I see it, you have a 100% chance of being happy by taking even money or a 69.26% of being happy by refusing it.

A: If you want long-term success, whether in the casino or real life, you sometimes have to take educated risks for long-term gain. Those who live only for the present are usually not as successful as those who know how to delay gratification.

Q: What is your opinion of betting two columns in roulette? Wouldn't this give me a 63.16% chance of winning? It seems to me it can't lose.

A: Yes, you have a 63.16% chance of winning. But you are risking $2 to win $1. You need to win over 66.67% of your roulette bets to come out ahead given this scenario.

Q: *What do you think of the mimic-the-dealer strategy (play your hand according to the dealer's hit/stand rules) in blackjack? The odds appear to be 50/50, except the player wins 3-2 on a black-jack while the dealer wins only even money. How could all the black-jack experts have overlooked this?*

A: You're forgetting that if both you and the dealer bust, you lose. Mimic the dealer is a terrible strategy, resulting in a house edge of 5.48%.

Q: *In the game of Sic Bo, I choose a number, 5 for example. Three dice are rolled. If one 5 is rolled I win even money, two 5s pays 2-1, and three 5s pays 3-1. Since the probability of rolling at least one 5 is (1/6) + (1/6) + (1/6) = 3/6, this must have a player advantage since the average payoff is more than even money. Is there a flaw in my logic, or should I sell my house and head to Vegas?*

A: Don't sell your house just yet. The flaw in your log-ic is that you should multiply probabilities, not add them. The probability of getting at least one five in three dice is 1-(5/6)x(5/6)x(5/6) = 42.13%. If you don't believe me, then by your logic the odds of rolling at least one five with six dice would be 100%, and it's obvious that that's impossible. The house edge on this bet is 7.87%.

Q: *As you know, there is a long-standing debate between the math geeks and the old-school gambling experts about splitting 8s against a ten in blackjack. Your camp argues that the player loses less money by splitting. The flaw in your argument is that you don't consider that the player has to bet more when splitting. He may have a smaller losing percentage, but it's applied to a larger bet.*

A: The fact that a player has to bet more when splitting is fully considered by basic strategy, which tells us to split the 8s. Given a $10 bet in a 6-deck game after considering all possible outcomes, the player can expect to lose $5.35 by hitting and $4.76 by splitting, across all money bet. The basic strategies contained in this book and those of other legitimate gambling writers are 100% accurate at maximizing the player's return. Mathematical models and computer simulations don't lie and they always come up with the same result.

Q: Have you heard of the "flaw" in the blackjack basic strategy? I've heard that the original creator of the basic strategy made a mistake, which has been passed down from blackjack book to blackjack book ever since. Only a few people know what the flaw is, but won't provide specifics.

A: This seems to be a new gambling urban legend that, not surprisingly, is being spread through bulletin boards by those searching for the holy grail of betting systems. The basic strategy was not created just once, but many times independently, including by myself. The results for a given set of rules are always the same.

Q: Why are the basic strategy and house edge in blackjack different depending on the number of decks? If I'm not counting cards, what difference does it make?

A: As each card leaves the deck, it affects the distribution of the remaining cards. The fewer the decks, the greater this effect becomes. Even if you don't count cards, this effect still exists. Here's an example. With two 7s against a dealer ten in a single-deck game, the correct play is to stand — an unthinkable play in a multiple-deck game. The reason is that with only one deck, two of the four 7s have already been removed. If the dealer gets a 20, the only single draw that will beat it is another 7. With half the sevens already gone, the value of hitting is substantially reduced, leaving standing as the better play by default. The reason the house edge is lower in a single-deck game is largely because a single deck game results in more stiff hands, and the player has the option to stand on a stiff hand while the dealer is forced to hit. There are also more blackjacks, and doubles and splits become more valuable as the number of decks goes down.

Q: Does a bad player at third base cause all players at the table to lose?

A: Of course, in the short run, the last player to act can indirectly cause the entire table to win or lose by making a bad play. However, over the long run, the third-baseman's strategy doesn't matter. He's just as likely to help you with an incorrect play as hurt you.

Q: Are my odds better or worse by playing multiple hands at blackjack?

A: They're the same.

Q: Which seat in blackjack offers the best odds?

A: They're all equal.

Q: If I buy a lottery ticket, what is more likely to win? 1-2-3-4-5-6 or a quick pick?

A: They are equally likely.

Q: Are video poker and video keno games fair?

A: Speaking for the major American-made brands, like

IGT, Williams, and Bally's, yes. It's Nevada state law that video representations of cards be dealt fairly and randomly, and most other jurisdictions tend to mirror Nevada gaming laws. As far as I know, the slot makers adhere to the same rule for video keno. An exception is spinning wheels, which may be engineered so that some outcomes (generally the lower paying) are more likely than others—for example, bonus wheels on some slot machines and blackjack side bets.

Appendix A

Blackjack Basic Strategies

TABLE 54—Single Deck, Dealer Stands on Soft 17

Your hand	Dealer's card 2	3	4	5	6	7	8	9	10	A
8	H	H	H	D	D	H	H	H	H	H
9	D	D	D	D	D	H	H	H	H	H
10	D	D	D	D	D	D	D	D	H	H
11	D	D	D	D	D	D	D	D	D	D
12	H	H	S	S	S	H	H	H	H	H
13	S	S	S	S	S	H	H	H	H	H
14	S	S	S	S	S	H	H	H	H	H
15	S	S	S	S	S	H	H	H	H	H
16	S	S	S	S	S	H	H	H	R/H	R/H
17	S	S	S	S	S	S	S	S	S	S
A,2	H	H	D	D	D	H	H	H	H	H
A,3	H	H	D	D	D	H	H	H	H	H
A,4	H	H	D	D	D	H	H	H	H	H
A,5	H	H	D	D	D	H	H	H	H	H
A,6	D	D	D	D	D	H	H	H	H	H
A,7	S	D/S	D/S	D/S	D/S	S	S	H	H	S
A,8	S	S	S	S	D/S	S	S	S	S	S
2,2	P/H	P	P	P	P	P	H	H	H	H
3,3	P/H	P/H	P	P	P	P	P/H	H	H	H
4,4	H	H	P/H	P/D	P/D	H	H	H	H	H
5,5	D	D	D	D	D	D	D	D	H	H
6,6	P	P	P	P	P	P/H	H	H	H	H
7,7	P	P	P	P	P	P	P/H	H	R/S	H
8,8	P	P	P	P	P	P	P	P	P	P
9,9	P	P	P	P	P	S	P	P	S	S
10,10	S	S	S	S	S	S	S	S	S	S
A,A	P	P	P	P	P	P	P	P	P	P

See key next page.

TABLE 55—Single Deck, Dealer Hits on Soft 17

Your hand	Dealer's card									
	2	3	4	5	6	7	8	9	10	A
8	H	H	H	D	D	H	H	H	H	H
9	D	D	D	D	D	H	H	H	H	H
10	D	D	D	D	D	D	D	D	H	H
11	D	D	D	D	D	D	D	D	D	D
12	H	H	S	S	S	H	H	H	H	H
13	S	S	S	S	S	H	H	H	H	H
14	S	S	S	S	S	H	H	H	H	H
15	S	S	S	S	S	H	H	H	H	R/H
16	S	S	S	S	S	H	H	H	R/H	R/H
17	S	S	S	S	S	S	S	S	S	R/S
A,2	H	H	D	D	D	H	H	H	H	H
A,3	H	H	D	D	D	H	H	H	H	H
A,4	H	H	D	D	D	H	H	H	H	H
A,5	H	H	D	D	D	H	H	H	H	H
A,6	D	D	D	D	D	H	H	H	H	H
A,7	S	D/S	D/S	D/S	D/S	S	S	H	H	H
A,8	S	S	S	S	D/S	S	S	S	S	S
2,2	P/H	P	P	P	P	P	H	H	H	H
3,3	P/H	P/H	P	P	P	P	P/H	H	H	H
4,4	H	H	P/H	P/D	P/D	H	H	H	H	H
5,5	D	D	D	D	D	D	D	D	H	H
6,6	P	P	P	P	P	P/H	H	H	H	H
7,7	P	P	P	P	P	P	P/H	H	R/S	R/H
8,8	P	P	P	P	P	P	P	P	P	P
9,9	P	P	P	P	P	S	P	P	S	P/S
10,10	S	S	S	S	S	S	S	S	S	S
A,A	P	P	P	P	P	P	P	P	P	P

Key to Tables

H Hit
S Stand
D Double if allowed, otherwise hit
D/S Double if allowed, otherwise stand
P Split
P/H Split if allowed to double after a split, otherwise hit
P/D Split if allowed to double after a split, otherwise double
P/S Split if allowed to double after a split, otherwise stand
R/H Surrender if allowed, otherwise hit
R/S Surrender if allowed, otherwise stand
R/P Surrender if allowed, otherwise split

TABLE 56—Double Deck, Dealer Stands on Soft 17

Your hand	Dealer's card									
	2	3	4	5	6	7	8	9	10	A
8	H	H	H	H	H	H	H	H	H	H
9	D	D	D	D	D	H	H	H	H	H
10	D	D	D	D	D	D	D	D	H	H
11	D	D	D	D	D	D	D	D	D	D
12	H	H	S	S	S	H	H	H	H	H
13	S	S	S	S	S	H	H	H	H	H
14	S	S	S	S	S	H	H	H	H	H
15	S	S	S	S	S	H	H	H	R/H	H
16	S	S	S	S	S	H	H	H	R/H	R/H
17	S	S	S	S	S	S	S	S	S	S
A,2	H	H	H	D	D	H	H	H	H	H
A,3	H	H	H	D	D	H	H	H	H	H
A,4	H	H	D	D	D	H	H	H	H	H
A,5	H	H	D	D	D	H	H	H	H	H
A,6	H	D	D	D	D	H	H	H	H	H
A,7	S	D/S	D/S	D/S	D/S	S	S	H	H	H
A,8	S	S	S	S	S	S	S	S	S	S
2,2	P/H	P/H	P	P	P	P	H	H	H	H
3,3	P/H	P/H	P	P	P	P	H	H	H	H
4,4	H	H	H	P/H	P/H	H	H	H	H	H
5,5	D	D	D	D	D	D	D	D	H	H
6,6	P	P	P	P	P	P/H	H	H	H	H
7,7	P	P	P	P	P	P	P/H	H	H	H
8,8	P	P	P	P	P	P	P	P	P	P
9,9	P	P	P	P	P	S	P	P	S	S
10,10	S	S	S	S	S	S	S	S	S	S
A,A	P	P	P	P	P	P	P	P	P	P

TABLE 57—Double Deck, Dealer Hits on Soft 17

Your hand	Dealer's card									
	2	3	4	5	6	7	8	9	10	A
8	H	H	H	H	H	H	H	H	H	H
9	D	D	D	D	D	H	H	H	H	H
10	D	D	D	D	D	D	D	D	H	H
11	D	D	D	D	D	D	D	D	D	D
12	H	H	S	S	S	H	H	H	H	H
13	S	S	S	S	S	H	H	H	H	H
14	S	S	S	S	S	H	H	H	H	H
15	S	S	S	S	S	H	H	H	R/H	R/H
16	S	S	S	S	S	H	H	H	R/H	R/H
17	S	S	S	S	S	S	S	S	S	R/S
A,2	H	H	H	D	D	H	H	H	H	H
A,3	H	H	D	D	D	H	H	H	H	H
A,4	H	H	D	D	D	H	H	H	H	H
A,5	H	H	D	D	D	H	H	H	H	H
A,6	H	D	D	D	D	H	H	H	H	H
A,7	D/S	D/S	D/S	D/S	D/S	S	S	H	H	H
A,8	S	S	S	S	D/S	S	S	S	S	S
2,2	P/H	P/H	P	P	P	P	H	H	H	H
3,3	P/H	P/H	P	P	P	P	H	H	H	H
4,4	H	H	H	P/H	P/H	H	H	H	H	H
5,5	D	D	D	D	D	D	D	D	H	H
6,6	P	P	P	P	P	P/H	H	H	H	H
7,7	P	P	P	P	P	P	P/H	H	H	H
8,8	P	P	P	P	P	P	P	P	P	P
9,9	P	P	P	P	P	S	P	P	S	S
10,10	S	S	S	S	S	S	S	S	S	S
A,A	P	P	P	P	P	P	P	P	P	P

Key to Tables

H Hit
S Stand
D Double if allowed, otherwise hit
D/S Double if allowed, otherwise stand
P Split
P/H Split if allowed to double after a split, otherwise hit
P/D Split if allowed to double after a split, otherwise double
P/S Split if allowed to double after a split, otherwise stand
R/H Surrender if allowed, otherwise hit
R/S Surrender if allowed, otherwise stand
R/P Surrender if allowed, otherwise split

TABLE 58—4 to 8 Deck, Dealer Stands on Soft 17

Your hand	2	3	4	5	6	7	8	9	10	A
				Dealer's card						
5-8	H	H	H	H	H	H	H	H	H	H
9	H	D	D	D	D	H	H	H	H	H
10	D	D	D	D	D	D	D	D	H	H
11	D	D	D	D	D	D	D	D	D	H
12	H	H	S	S	S	H	H	H	H	H
13	S	S	S	S	S	H	H	H	H	H
14	S	S	S	S	S	H	H	H	H	H
15	S	S	S	S	S	H	H	H	R/H	H
16	S	S	S	S	S	H	H	R/H	R/H	R/H
17	S	S	S	S	S	S	S	S	S	S
A,2	H	H	H	D	D	H	H	H	H	H
A,3	H	H	H	D	D	H	H	H	H	H
A,4	H	H	D	D	D	H	H	H	H	H
A,5	H	H	D	D	D	H	H	H	H	H
A,6	H	D	D	D	D	H	H	H	H	H
A,7	S	D/S	D/S	D/S	D/S	S	S	H	H	H
A,8	S	S	S	S	S	S	S	S	S	S
2,2	P/H	P/H	P	P	P	P	H	H	H	H
3,3	P/H	P/H	P	P	P	P	H	H	H	H
4,4	H	H	H	P/H	P/H	H	H	H	H	H
5,5	D	D	D	D	D	D	D	D	H	H
6,6	P/H	P	P	P	P	H	H	H	H	H
7,7	P	P	P	P	P	P	H	H	H	H
8,8	P	P	P	P	P	P	P	P	P	P
9,9	P	P	P	P	P	S	P	P	S	S
10,10	S	S	S	S	S	S	S	S	S	S
A,A	P	P	P	P	P	P	P	P	P	P

TABLE 59—4 to 8 Deck, Dealer Hits on Soft 17

Your hand	Dealer's card 2	3	4	5	6	7	8	9	10	A
8	H	H	H	H	H	H	H	H	H	H
9	H	D	D	D	D	H	H	H	H	H
10	D	D	D	D	D	D	D	D	H	H
11	D	D	D	D	D	D	D	D	D	D
12	H	H	S	S	S	H	H	H	H	H
13	S	S	S	S	S	H	H	H	H	H
14	S	S	S	S	S	H	H	H	H	H
15	S	S	S	S	S	H	H	H	R/H	R/H
16	S	S	S	S	S	H	H	R/H	R/H	R/H
17	S	S	S	S	S	S	S	S	S	R/S
A,2	H	H	H	D	D	H	H	H	H	H
A,3	H	H	H	D	D	H	H	H	H	H
A,4	H	H	D	D	D	H	H	H	H	H
A,5	H	H	D	D	D	H	H	H	H	H
A,6	H	D	D	D	D	H	H	H	H	H
A,7	D/S	D/S	D/S	D/S	D/S	S	S	H	H	H
A,8	S	S	S	S	D/S	S	S	S	S	S
2,2	P/H	P/H	P	P	P	P	H	H	H	H
3,3	P/H	P/H	P	P	P	P	H	H	H	H
4,4	H	H	H	P/H	P/H	H	H	H	H	H
5,5	D	D	D	D	D	D	D	D	H	H
6,6	P/H	P	P	P	P	H	H	H	H	H
7,7	P	P	P	P	P	P	H	H	H	H
8,8	P	P	P	P	P	P	P	P	P	R/P
9,9	P	P	P	P	P	S	P	P	S	S
10,10	S	S	S	S	S	S	S	S	S	S
A,A	P	P	P	P	P	P	P	P	P	P

Key to Tables

H Hit
S Stand
D Double if allowed, otherwise hit
D/S Double if allowed, otherwise stand
P Split
P/H Split if allowed to double after a split, otherwise hit
P/D Split if allowed to double after a split, otherwise double
P/S Split if allowed to double after a split, otherwise stand
R/H Surrender if allowed, otherwise hit
R/S Surrender if allowed, otherwise stand
R/P Surrender if allowed, otherwise split

Appendix B

Spanish 21 Basic Strategies

TABLE 60—Basic Strategy for Spanish 21
Dealer Hits on Soft 17, No Redoubling

	2	3	4	5	6	7	8	9	10	A
9	H	H	H	H	D	H	H	H	H	H
10	D5	D5	D	D	D	D4	D3	H	H	H
11	D4	D5	D5	D5	D5	D4	D4	D4	D3	D3
12	H	H	H	H	H	H	H	H	H	H
13	H	H	H	H	S4*	H	H	H	H	H
14	H	H	S4*	S5'	S6"	H	H	H	H	H
15	S4*	S5'	S6	S6	S	H	H	H	H	H
16	S6	S6	S6	S	S	H	H	H	H	Rh
17	S	S	S	S	S	S	S6	S6	S6	Rh
A,2	H	H	H	H	H	H	H	H	H	H
A,3	H	H	H	H	H	H	H	H	H	H
A,4	H	H	H	H	D4	H	H	H	H	H
A,5	H	H	H	D3	D4	H	H	H	H	H
A,6	H	H	D3	D4	D5	H	H	H	H	H
A,7	S4	S4	D4	D5	D6	S6	S4	H	H	H
A,8	S	S	S	S	S	S	S	S	S6	S6
2,2	P	P	P	P	P	P	H	H	H	H
3,3	P	P	P	P	P	P	P	H	H	H
6,6	H	H	P	P	P	H	H	H	H	H
7,7	P	P	P	P	P	P$	H	H	H	H
8,8	P	P	P	P	P	P	P	P	P	R
9,9	S	P	P	P	P	S	P	P	S	S
A,A	P	P	P	P	P	P	P	P	P	P

Double down surrender: 12-16 vs 8-A, 17 vs A
Never split 4's, 5's, or 10's

See Key Page 134

TABLE 61—Basic Strategy for Spanish 21
Dealer Stands on Soft 17, No Redoubling

	2	3	4	5	6	7	8	9	10	A
9	H	H	H	H	D3	H	H	H	H	H
10	D5	D5	D	D	D	D4	D3	H	H	H
11	D4	D5	D5	D5	D5	D4	D4	D4	D3	D3
12	H	H	H	H	H	H	H	H	H	H
13	H	H	H	H	H	H	H	H	H	H
14	H	H	S4*	S5*	S4*	H	H	H	H	H
15	S4*	S5*	S5"	S6	S6	H	H	H	H	H
16	S5	S6	S6	S	S	H	H	H	H	H
17	S	S	S	S	S	S	S6	S6	S6	Rh
A,2	H	H	H	H	H	H	H	H	H	H
A,3	H	H	H	H	H	H	H	H	H	H
A,4	H	H	H	H	H	H	H	H	H	H
A,5	H	H	H	H	D4	H	H	H	H	H
A,6	H	H	D3	D4	D5	H	H	H	H	H
A,7	S4	S4	D4	D5	D5	S6	S4	H	H	H
A,8	S	S	S	S	S	S	S	S	S6	S
2,2	P	P	P	P	P	P	H	H	H	H
3,3	P	P	P	P	P	P	P	H	H	H
6,6	H	H	P	P	P	H	H	H	H	H
7,7	P	P	P	P	P	P$	H	H	H	H
8,8	P	P	P	P	P	P	P	P	P	P
9,9	S	P	P	P	P	S	P	P	S	S
A,A	P	P	P	P	P	P	P	P	P	P

Double down surrender: 12-16 vs 8-A, 17 vs A
Never split 4's, 5's, or 10's

See Key Page 134

TABLE 62—Basic Strategy for Spanish 21
Dealer Hits on Soft 17, Redoubling Allowed

	2	3	4	5	6	7	8	9	10	A
5	H	H	H	H	D	H	H	H	H	H
6	H	H	H	H	D	H	H	H	H	H
7	H	H	H	H	D	H	H	H	H	H
8	H	H	H	D	D	H	H	H	H	H
9	H	D4	D	D	D	H	H	H	H	H
10	D5	D5	D	D	D	D4	D3	H	H	H
11	D4	D5	D5	D5	D5	D4	D4	D4	D3	D3
12	H	H	H	H	H	H	H	H	H	H
13	H	H	H	H	S4*	H	H	H	H	H
14	H	H	S4*	S5′	S6″	H	H	H	H	H
15	S4*	S5′	S6	S6	S	H	H	H	H	H
16	S6	S6	S6	S	S	H	H	H	H	Rh
17	S	S	S	S	S	S	S6	S6	S6	Rh
A,2	H	D	D	D	D	H	H	H	H	H
A,3	H	D3	D	D	D	H	H	H	H	H
A,4	H	H	D4	D4	D5	H	H	H	H	H
A,5	H	H	D3	D4	D5	H	H	H	H	H
A,6	H	H	D3	D4	D5	H	H	H	H	H
A,7	S4	S4	D4	D5	D6	S6	S4	H	H	H
A,8	S	S	S	S	S	S	S	S	S6	S6
2,2	P	P	P	P	P	P	P	H	H	H
3,3	P	P	P	P	P	P	P	H	H	H
6,6	H	H	P	P	P	H	H	H	H	H
7,7	P	P	P	P	P	P$	H	H	H	H
8,8	P	P	P	P	P	P	P	P	P	R
9,9	S	P	P	P	P	S	P	P	S	S
A,A	P	P	P	P	P	P	P	P	P	P

Double down surrender: 12-16 vs 8-A, 17 vs A
Never split 4's, 5's, or 10's

See Key Page 134

Key to tables

H	Hit
S	Stand
D	Double
P	Split
R	Surrender
Rh	Surrender on first two cards, otherwise hit
S3	Stand, unless hand is composed of 3 or more cards then hit
S4	Stand, unless hand is composed of 4 or more cards then hit
S5	Stand, unless hand is composed of 5 or more cards then hit
S6	Stand, unless hand is composed of 6 or more cards then hit
D3	Double, unless hand is composed of 3 or more cards then hit
D4	Double, unless hand is composed of 4 or more cards then hit
D5	Double, unless hand is composed of 5 or more cards then hit
D6	Double, unless hand is composed of 6 or more cards then hit
*	Hit if any 6-7-8 bonus possible
'	Hit if suited or spaded 6-7-8 bonus is possible
"	Hit if spaded 6-7-8 bonus is possible
$	Hit if two sevens are suited (possible super bonus)

Match the Dealer

In some locations there is a side bet available if either or both of the player's first two cards match the dealer's up card. In a six-deck game a non-suited match pays 4 to 1 and a suited match pays 9 to 1. In an eight-deck game a non-suited match pays 3 to 1 and a suited match pays 12 to 1. The side bet has a house edge of 3.06% in the six-deck game, and 2.99% in the eight-deck game.

Appendix C

Keno $1 9-Spot Returns in Las Vegas

TABLE 63—Keno Payback Comparison—Las Vegas

Casino	Return	Casino	Return
Silverton	79.85%	Western	70.80%
Arizona Charlie's	75.13%	Western	70.35%
Frontier	74.83%	Luxor	70.23%
Jerry's Nugget	74.78%	Circus Circus	70.23%
Nevada Palace	74.62%	Main Street Station	70.12%
Orleans	74.39%	California	70.12%
Gold Coast	74.39%	Riviera	69.66%
Sam's Town	74.28%	Stardust	69.44%
Las Vegas Club	72.82%	Plaza	69.18%
Rio	72.76%	San Remo	69.08%
Mirage	71.87%	Aladdin	68.52%
Bellagio	71.87%	Fremont	68.52%
Golden Nugget	71.38%	Four Queens	68.52%
MGM Grand	71.13%	Bally's	68.17%
New York-New York	71.13%	Treasure Island	67.54%
Primm Valley Resorts	70.86%	Caesars Palace	67.54%
Hilton	70.80%	Station Casinos	66.54%
Fitzgeralds	70.80%	Palms	66.24%
Binion's Horseshoe	70.80%		

Appendix D

Pai Gow Poker
House-Way Strategy

The casino house ways for setting pai gow poker hand vary slightly from one to another. Here's an example of one house way currently in use.

No pair: Place the highest card in the high hand and the next two highest cards in the low hand.

One pair: Place the pair in the high hand and the next two highest cards in the low hand.

Two pair: Play the high pair in the high hand, except play the two pair together with any of the following:

Two low pairs (2-6) and a king or ace singleton.

Low pair and medium pair (7-10) and a king or ace singleton.

Low pair and high pair (J-K) and an ace singleton.

Two medium pairs and an ace singleton

Three pair: Always play highest pair in the low hand.

Three-of-a-kind: Keep together, except split apart three aces.

Straights, flushes, straight flushes:

With no pair: Retain the straight/flush/straight flush in the high hand. If more than one is possible then play the one that results in the highest possible low hand.

With one pair: Play pair in the low hand only if a straight, flush, or straight flush can be retained in the high hand.

With two pair: Use two pair rule.

With three pair: Use three pair rule.

With three of a kind: Play pair in the low hand.

With full house: Use full house rule.

Full house: Always split unless the pair is twos and you have an ace and a king to play in the low hand.

Full house with three of a kind and two pairs: Play the higher pair in the low hand.

Full house with three of a kind twice: Play a pair from the higher three of a kind in the low hand.

Four-of-a-kind: Play according to the rank of the four of a kind:

2 through 6: Always keep together.

7 through 10: Split unless a king or better can be played in the low hand.

Jack through king: Split unless an ace can be played in the low hand.

Aces: Always split.

Four-of-a-kind and a pair: Play pair in the low hand.

Four-of-a-kind and three-of-a-kind: Play pair in the low hand from the three-of-a-kind.

Five aces: If you don't have a pair of kings, then split the aces apart, playing a pair of aces in the low hand. If you do have a pair of kings, then play five aces in high hand and kings in the low hand.

Appendix E

Slot Machine
Return Percentages

The following was originally published as an article titled "The Slot Payout Comparison" in the May 2002 issue of the *Las Vegas Advisor*.

One of the last casino mysteries is the return percentages of slot machines. In all other casino games, the rules are disclosed or observable and the house edge can be determined. However, slots are controlled by computer microchips and random-number generators, and unless the player knows how the machine was programmed, there's no way to determine the theoretical return. After analyzing all the major casino games and many obscure ones, the slot machine was my personal final frontier.

Before going further, let's define "slot machine." A slot machine is a gambling device with actual, or video representations of, spinning reels. This does not include video poker, video keno, or video blackjack. Confusion often arises when sources report slot payback percentages that include all gaming machines, including video poker. It's important to understand that those rankings are for slot machines only.

The problem with slots is that the information needed to analyze them isn't easily obtained. Slot managers have always kept their slot-return percentages top secret. And I've asked several major slot makers for the specifications to their machines (called "PAR sheets"), but they've always refused. Luckily, a fan of my Web site who had access to PAR sheets gave me what I needed to do the work.

A given machine can have multiple PAR sheets, each with a selection of return percentages. So simply having the sheets didn't tell me which applied to which machine or casino. But using the PAR sheets for multi-line video-display slot machines, I was able to identify certain combinations of symbols that narrowed down the possibilities. Then, by using my findings as a map and playing in each casino, I was able to determine the exact return percentage for each location. (The complete methodology is more complicated and is explained in more detail on my Web site.)

I spent hundreds of hours going from casino to casino, looking for the right games, playing them, and recording the results. I canvassed many casinos multiple times, as I added more varieties of slots to my survey, which made for a larger and more representative sample. The vast majority of video-display slots I encountered were 5¢ denominated, so the entire survey is based on nickel machines. Keep in mind that a reliable rule of thumb tells us that higher denominations have higher return percentages. While this report does not make claims about returns on machines other than nickels, I suspect we can infer a great deal about across-the-board percentages based on the nickel ranking.

The table that follows ranks the return from nickel slots at 71 Las Vegas casinos [this list includes additional entries and a few updates from the list that was originally published]. There seemed to be no truth to slot-placement myths. That is, machines on the end of a bank (or row) did no better, on average, than those in the middle. There was also no correlation between return and proximity to such things as the main door, table-game pit, or high-or low-traffic areas.

Most casinos were consistent in their returns. If one nickel machine had a return of x%, then all others like it also returned x%. However, some casinos did mix loose and tight machines, most notably Treasure Island and the California.

TABLE 64—Slot-Return Comparison—Las Vegas

Rank	Casino	Return	Rank	Casino	Return
1	Palms	93.42%	37	Casino Royale	91.67%
2	Gold Coast	92.84%	38	Boulder Station	91.55%
3	Sahara	92.81%	39	Aladdin	91.50%
4	Bourbon Street	92.63%	40	O'Sheas	91.48%
4	Imperial Palace	92.63%	41	Hilton	91.40%
4	Slots A Fun	92.63%	42	Boardwalk	91.28%
7	Key Largo (now closed)	92.60%	43	New York-New York	90.99%
8	Western	92.57%	44	Horseshoe	90.96%
9	Circus Circus	92.56%	45	Sam's Town	90.89%
9	El Cortez	92.56%	46	Santa Fe Station	90.87%
9	Ellis Island	92.56%	47	Flamingo	90.86%
9	Orleans	92.56%	48	Golden Nugget	90.85%
13	Gold Spike	92.55%	49	Stratosphere	90.80%
14	Fitzgeralds	92.54%	50	Tropicana	90.71%
15	Fiesta Rancho	92.53%	51	Golden Gate	90.64%
16	Arizona Charlie's East	92.51%	52	Silverton	90.57%
17	Barbary Coast	92.50%	53	Main Street Station	90.56%
18	Arizona Charlie's West	92.49%	54	Westward Ho	90.40%
18	Terrible's	92.49%	55	Fremont	90.37%
20	Hard Rock	92.47%	56	Castaways (now closed)	90.36%
20	Longhorn	92.47%	57	Monte Carlo	90.24%
20	Townhall (now closed)	92.47%	58	Stardust	89.97%
23	Riviera	92.23%	59	Frontier	89.91%
24	California	92.14%	60	MGM Grand	89.81%
25	Lady Luck	92.10%	61	Harrah's	89.32%
26	Nevada Palace	92.06%	61	Treasure Island	89.32%
27	Plaza	91.94%	63	Mirage	89.30%
28	Luxor	91.92%	64	Caesars Palace	89.05%
28	Paris	91.92%	65	Mandalay Bay	88.87%
30	San Remo	91.88%	66	Rio	88.72%
31	Excalibur	91.84%	67	La Bayou	88.26%
31	Palace Station	91.84%	67	Mermaids	88.26%
33	Bally's	91.82%	69	Bellagio	87.42%
34	Las Vegas Club	91.76%	70	Venetian	86.66%
35	Four Queens	91.75%	71	Airport	85.02%
36	Texas Station	91.71%			

Note: The Suncoast, Rampart, and Fiesta Henderson are not included in the survey for not allowing me to play and take notes at the same time.

Appendix F

Probabilities of Winning Hands in Texas Hold 'Em

Table 65 ranks all the possible 2-card starting hands, from best to worst, in a 10-player game (including yourself). The table assumes that all players stay in until the end of the hand. Following is an explanation of each column.

Cards – Your starting two cards.

Probability of Win – The probability of winning the hand.

Average Win – Number of units you expect to win (including your own bets). This is less than 10 units, because there's always a chance of tying and splitting the pot.

Expected Value – A measure of how much the hand is worth. For example, if you have a pair of aces and expect everyone to bet $100 on the hand, then the hand is worth $210.97.

Probability of Hand – This is the probability of getting this hand in the first place.

Additive Probability – The probability of getting this hand or any better hand. For example, if you wish to play on the top 20% of hands then you should play an unsuited Jack/10 or better, which accounts for the top 20.21% of hands.

TABLE 65—Starting-Hand Order in 10-Player Texas Hold 'Em Game

Cards	Probability of Win	Average Win	Expected Value	Probability of Hand	Additive Probability
Pair of A's	31.38%	9.91	2.1097	0.45%	0.45%
Pair of K's	26.43%	9.87	1.6089	0.45%	0.90%
Pair of Q's	22.67%	9.81	1.2233	0.45%	1.36%
A/K suited	21.71%	9.52	1.0672	0.3%	1.66%
Pair of J's	19.88%	9.74	0.9352	0.45%	2.11%
A/Q suited	20.46%	9.42	0.9265	0.3%	2.41%
K/Q suited	19.77%	9.41	0.8617	0.3%	2.71%
A/J suited	19.53%	9.31	0.8176	0.3%	3.02%
K/J suited	18.91%	9.31	0.7613	0.3%	3.32%
A/T suited	18.87%	9.2	0.7364	0.3%	3.62%
A/K unsuited	18.28%	9.41	0.7204	0.9%	4.52%
Q/J suited	18.53%	9.29	0.7203	0.3%	4.83%
Pair of T's	17.77%	9.66	0.7163	0.45%	5.28%
K/T suited	18.37%	9.21	0.6915	0.3%	5.58%
J/T suited	18.07%	9.17	0.6562	0.3%	5.88%
Q/T suited	18.02%	9.19	0.6553	0.3%	6.18%
Pair of 9's	16.04%	9.69	0.5546	0.45%	6.64%
A/Q unsuited	16.78%	9.26	0.5541	0.9%	7.54%
A/9 suited	16.89%	9.11	0.5393	0.3%	7.84%
K/Q unsuited	16.29%	9.26	0.5095	0.9%	8.75%
T/9 suited	16.32%	9.1	0.4847	0.3%	9.05%
K/9 suited	16.21%	9.15	0.4833	0.3%	9.35%
A/8 suited	16.36%	9.03	0.478	0.3%	9.65%
J/9 suited	15.95%	9.12	0.4548	0.3%	9.95%
Q/9 suited	15.9%	9.14	0.4535	0.3%	10.26%
Pair of 8's	15%	9.67	0.4509	0.45%	10.71%
A/5 suited	16.23%	8.9	0.4443	0.3%	11.01%
A/J unsuited	15.71%	9.1	0.4295	0.9%	11.92%
A/7 suited	15.93%	8.96	0.4268	0.3%	12.22%
A/4 suited	15.9%	8.94	0.4217	0.3%	12.52%
A/3 suited	15.51%	9	0.3954	0.3%	12.82%
K/J unsuited	15.3%	9.11	0.3944	0.9%	13.73%
A/6 suited	15.63%	8.91	0.3935	0.3%	14.03%
Q/J unsuited	15.06%	9.08	0.3683	0.9%	14.93%
Pair of 7's	14.15%	9.65	0.3653	0.45%	15.38%
K/8 suited	15.03%	9.03	0.358	0.3%	15.69%
A/2 suited	15.01%	9.04	0.3574	0.3%	15.99%
T/8 suited	15.04%	9	0.3546	0.3%	16.29%

9/8 suited	14.7%	9.11	0.3391	0.3%	16.59%
A/T unsuited	14.93%	8.94	0.3351	0.9%	17.50%
J/8 suited	14.69%	9.03	0.326	0.3%	17.80%
Q/8 suited	14.59%	9.04	0.3184	0.3%	18.10%
K/7 suited	14.66%	8.96	0.3126	0.3%	18.40%
K/T unsuited	14.6%	8.96	0.3085	0.9%	19.31%
J/T unsuited	14.65%	8.92	0.307	0.9%	20.21%
Pair of 6's	13.5%	9.63	0.3004	0.45%	20.66%
Q/T unsuited	14.45%	8.94	0.2921	0.9%	21.57%
K/6 suited	14.31%	8.91	0.2749	0.3%	21.87%
8/7 suited	14.01%	9.08	0.2719	0.3%	22.17%
K/5 suited	14.11%	8.87	0.2518	0.3%	22.47%
9/7 suited	13.79%	9.04	0.2471	0.3%	22.78%
Pair of 5's	12.89%	9.61	0.2388	0.45%	23.23%
T/7 suited	13.83%	8.91	0.2317	0.3%	23.53%
K/4 suited	13.79%	8.92	0.2309	0.3%	23.83%
7/6 suited	13.52%	9.06	0.2247	0.3%	24.13%
Pair of 4's	12.57%	9.68	0.2166	0.45%	24.59%
K/3 suited	13.47%	8.99	0.2107	0.3%	24.89%
Q/7 suited	13.56%	8.91	0.2085	0.3%	25.19%
J/7 suited	13.49%	8.91	0.2026	0.3%	25.49%
Pair of 3's	12.34%	9.75	0.2026	0.45%	25.94%
K/2 suited	13.18%	9.05	0.1932	0.3%	26.24%
Pair of 2's	12.14%	9.82	0.192	0.45%	26.70%
6/5 suited	13.16%	9.04	0.19	0.3%	27.00%
8/6 suited	13.19%	9.01	0.1886	0.3%	27.30%
Q/6 suited	13.27%	8.85	0.1752	0.3%	27.60%
5/4 suited	12.87%	9.04	0.1639	0.3%	27.90%
Q/5 suited	13.03%	8.82	0.149	0.3%	28.21%
7/5 suited	12.74%	8.99	0.1456	0.3%	28.51%
9/6 suited	12.72%	8.95	0.1391	0.3%	28.81%
T/9 unsuited	12.87%	8.8	0.1333	0.9%	29.71%
Q/4 suited	12.75%	8.87	0.1313	0.3%	30.02%
A/9 unsuited	12.76%	8.77	0.1187	0.9%	30.92%
T/6 suited	12.72%	8.79	0.118	0.3%	31.22%
Q/3 suited	12.45%	8.95	0.1141	0.3%	31.52%
6/4 suited	12.22%	9.07	0.1074	0.3%	31.83%
J/6 suited	12.55%	8.77	0.1015	0.3%	32.13%
Q/2 suited	12.18%	9.02	0.0993	0.3%	32.43%
J/9 unsuited	12.36%	8.81	0.0888	0.9%	33.33%
8/5 suited	12.17%	8.93	0.0861	0.3%	33.63%
5/3 suited	11.96%	9.07	0.0842	0.3%	33.94%
K/9 unsuited	12.26%	8.83	0.0827	0.9%	34.84%
J/5 suited	12.3%	8.74	0.075	0.3%	35.14%

Q/9 unsuited	12.1%	8.82	0.0674	0.9%	36.05%
J/4 suited	12.01%	8.8	0.057	0.3%	36.35%
A/8 unsuited	12.15%	8.63	0.0491	0.9%	37.25%
7/4 suited	11.59%	8.99	0.0425	0.3%	37.56%
J/3 suited	11.73%	8.88	0.041	0.3%	37.86%
4/3 suited	11.35%	9.13	0.036	0.3%	38.16%
9/5 suited	11.67%	8.85	0.032	0.3%	38.46%
J/2 suited	11.49%	8.95	0.0281	0.3%	38.76%
T/5 suited	11.84%	8.65	0.0248	0.3%	39.06%
A/5 unsuited	11.99%	8.44	0.0127	0.9%	39.97%
6/3 suited	11.1%	9.07	0.0071	0.3%	40.27%
T/4 suited	11.53%	8.7	0.0036	0.3%	40.57%
A/7 unsuited	11.7%	8.51	-0.0037	0.9%	41.48%
T/8 unsuited	11.47%	8.63	-0.0095	0.9%	42.38%
T/3 suited	11.24%	8.78	-0.0125	0.3%	42.68%
A/4 unsuited	11.62%	8.49	-0.0137	0.9%	43.59%
5/2 suited	10.84%	9.07	-0.0164	0.3%	43.89%
9/8 unsuited	11.18%	8.79	-0.0177	0.9%	44.80%
8/4 suited	11.03%	8.9	-0.0182	0.3%	45.10%
T/2 suited	10.96%	8.86	-0.0289	0.3%	45.40%
A/3 unsuited	11.21%	8.56	-0.0405	0.9%	46.30%
4/2 suited	10.47%	9.16	-0.0408	0.3%	46.61%
A/6 unsuited	11.34%	8.42	-0.0443	0.9%	47.51%
9/4 suited	10.73%	8.8	-0.0559	0.3%	47.81%
K/8 unsuited	10.97%	8.6	-0.056	0.9%	48.72%
J/8 unsuited	10.93%	8.63	-0.057	0.9%	49.62%
7/3 suited	10.47%	8.97	-0.06	0.3%	49.92%
9/3 suited	10.41%	8.87	-0.0768	0.3%	50.23%
Q/8 unsuited	10.7%	8.62	-0.0773	0.9%	51.13%
8/7 unsuited	10.58%	8.72	-0.0773	0.9%	52.04%
A/2 unsuited	10.71%	8.6	-0.0786	0.9%	52.94%
3/2 suited	9.91%	9.24	-0.084	0.3%	53.24%
9/2 suited	10.16%	8.96	-0.0901	0.3%	53.54%
6/2 suited	9.97%	9.06	-0.0959	0.3%	53.85%
K/7 unsuited	10.54%	8.48	-0.1067	0.9%	54.75%
8/3 suited	10.07%	8.86	-0.108	0.3%	55.05%
9/7 unsuited	10.23%	8.65	-0.1152	0.9%	55.96%
7/6 unsuited	10.1%	8.68	-0.1234	0.9%	56.86%
8/2 suited	9.79%	8.93	-0.1253	0.3%	57.16%
T/7 unsuited	10.17%	8.44	-0.1419	0.9%	58.07%
K/6 unsuited	10.18%	8.38	-0.1463	0.9%	58.97%
7/2 suited	9.52%	8.94	-0.1493	0.3%	59.28%
6/5 unsuited	9.74%	8.65	-0.1576	0.9%	60.18%
8/6 unsuited	9.68%	8.59	-0.1683	0.9%	61.09%

K/5 unsuited	9.92%	8.31	-0.1752	0.9%	61.99%
5/4 unsuited	9.5%	8.64	-0.1791	0.9%	62.90%
J/7 unsuited	9.67%	8.41	-0.1872	0.9%	63.80%
K/4 unsuited	9.59%	8.37	-0.1975	0.9%	64.71%
Q/7 unsuited	9.58%	8.36	-0.1991	0.9%	65.61%
7/5 unsuited	9.26%	8.55	-0.2085	0.9%	66.52%
K/3 unsuited	9.25%	8.45	-0.2178	0.9%	67.42%
9/6 unsuited	9.09%	8.46	-0.2305	0.9%	68.33%
K/2 unsuited	8.97%	8.54	-0.2341	0.9%	69.23%
Q/6 unsuited	9.25%	8.26	-0.236	0.9%	70.14%
6/4 unsuited	8.75%	8.63	-0.2442	0.9%	71.04%
Q/5 unsuited	9.01%	8.19	-0.2623	0.9%	71.95%
T/6 unsuited	8.98%	8.19	-0.2638	0.9%	72.85%
5/3 unsuited	8.52%	8.62	-0.2656	0.9%	73.76%
8/5 unsuited	8.58%	8.4	-0.2794	0.9%	74.66%
Q/4 unsuited	8.68%	8.26	-0.2836	0.9%	75.57%
J/6 unsuited	8.64%	8.13	-0.298	0.9%	76.47%
Q/3 unsuited	8.34%	8.35	-0.3037	0.9%	77.38%
4/3 unsuited	7.9%	8.69	-0.3135	0.9%	78.28%
7/4 unsuited	8.05%	8.48	-0.3176	0.9%	79.19%
Q/2 unsuited	8.07%	8.45	-0.3183	0.9%	80.09%
J/5 unsuited	8.4%	8.04	-0.3254	0.9%	81.00%
9/5 unsuited	7.99%	8.21	-0.3438	0.9%	81.90%
J/4 unsuited	8.06%	8.11	-0.3458	0.9%	82.81%
6/3 unsuited	7.56%	8.57	-0.3524	0.9%	83.71%
T/5 unsuited	8.07%	7.89	-0.3631	0.9%	84.62%
J/3 unsuited	7.76%	8.2	-0.3631	0.9%	85.52%
5/2 unsuited	7.34%	8.56	-0.3711	0.9%	86.43%
J/2 unsuited	7.48%	8.3	-0.3791	0.9%	87.33%
T/4 unsuited	7.7%	7.95	-0.3878	0.9%	88.24%
8/4 unsuited	7.38%	8.27	-0.3898	0.9%	89.14%
4/2 unsuited	6.95%	8.68	-0.3964	0.9%	90.05%
T/3 unsuited	7.4%	8.04	-0.4049	0.9%	90.95%
T/2 unsuited	7.11%	8.14	-0.4211	0.9%	91.86%
7/3 unsuited	6.85%	8.36	-0.4273	0.9%	92.76%
9/4 unsuited	6.96%	8.03	-0.4411	0.9%	93.67%
3/2 unsuited	6.35%	8.78	-0.4431	0.9%	94.57%
6/2 unsuited	6.39%	8.46	-0.4596	0.9%	95.48%
9/3 unsuited	6.63%	8.12	-0.4615	0.9%	96.38%
9/2 unsuited	6.36%	8.23	-0.4769	0.9%	97.29%
8/3 unsuited	6.36%	8.09	-0.485	0.9%	98.19%
8/2 unsuited	6.06%	8.19	-0.5038	0.9%	99.10%
7/2 unsuited	5.86%	8.18	-0.5209	0.9%	100%
Total	**11.33%**	**8.82**	**0**	**100.0%**	

Appendix G

Gambling Etiquette

The same standards for etiquette outside the casino also apply inside. Emotions can run the whole gamut in a casino, but regardless of whether you're on an extreme high, extreme low, or anywhere in between, you should still exercise common sense, restraint, and respect for others. That said, here are some etiquette tips that are specific to casinos.

- Don't correct or critique another player's play unless he's receptive to suggestions. In particular, don't harass the last player to act in blackjack. It's a myth that a bad player, particularly at third base, causes the entire table to lose.
- Be courteous to the dealers. It isn't their fault when you lose. If you can't take losing, then don't play at all.
- Tip the dealers. Dealers usually make minimum wage and rely on tips to make a decent living. Losing is not an excuse not to tip. Dealers should be tipped according to the level of service they provide. There is no firm standard, but I recommend tipping on average one-half your average bet per hour.
- Tip the cocktail waitresses. One dollar per drink is the standard. Ordering water does not excuse you from tipping.
- Tip slot personnel when you receive a hand-pay jackpot. It's touchy who should be tipped. In my opinion, you should tip whoever gives you the money plus anyone else

who provided a service to you while you played. As slots move more toward cashless this pertains to fewer people. Although some strongly disagree, I don't feel you need to pass out money to every tip vulture that hovers around your machine when the light goes off (indicating a hand-pay is imminent). In my opinion, for most pays tipping 1% to 2% is about right, depending on the amount and the speed in which paid.

• Do your best to understand rules and strategy before you play. Try not to slow down a game because you don't know how to play, unless you are the only one playing.

• If you make a bet using different chip denominations on a table game, put the higher denominations on the bottom of the stack.

• Once you make a bet in a table game, never touch it unless you win or push.

• Do not drink past the point where it annoys other people.

• I recognize that smokers have a right to smoke in casinos. However, if you must, try to do so in moderation. Between puffs hold the cigarette low, exhale in the direction of the least number of people, and when you put out the cigarette, put it out fully.

Appendix H

Resources

Blackjack

Basic Blackjack by Stanford Wong: The book is a study of the basic strategy and its adjustments under a host of different rules. Much of the book is devoted to analysis of short-term gimmicks that occurred in a limited area years ago. I would recommend this book to someone who plays a lot and may encounter unusual rules from time to time, including those who may play in Europe or Asia, or anyone with a mathematical interest in the game.

Blackbelt in Blackjack by Arnold Snyder: This is great A to Z book on card counting. I recommend it highly for beginning to intermediate counters. Snyder cuts quickly to the point on everything important to a card counter without being too technical or number heavy. Included is coverage of the Red Seven and Zen Counts.

Blackjack Attack by Don Schlesinger: This book is largely made up of Schlesinger's *Blackjack Forum* articles. Experienced players can gain a lot from one of the masters of blackjack theory, but it may be too advanced for beginning or intermediate players.

Blackjack Autumn – A True Tale of Life, Death, and Splitting Tens in Winnemucca by Barry Meadow: The story of one man's quest to count cards at every casino in Nevada. In one locale after another the writing is full of humorous similes and observations. A great page-turner, if not the most realistic depiction of serious card counting.

Blackjack Secrets by Stanford Wong: This book contains basics for beginners as well as fresh material for experienced players. This should not be your first book on blackjack or card counting, but I'm sure anyone at any level of expertise can learn a lot from it.

Blackjack Wisdom by Arnold Snyder: A collection of magazine articles by Synder. Fun and interesting reading for readers with a solid blackjack background. No charts or math-heavy analysis, just stories and talk about blackjack. A good bedside book.

Burning the Tables in Las Vegas by Ian Andersen: This is the follow-up to *Turning the Tables in Las Vegas*. In the 20 years since *Turning* was published, blackjack has changed and Andersen has a lot more advice to offer on player camouflage. At 305 pages, this book packs lots of information from topics varying from how to change your name to Chinese herbs that can sharpen your play. If you find yourself getting backed off or barred playing blackjack, this book may be just what you need.

Ken Uston on Blackjack by Ken Uston: Real stories from one of blackjack's best and most interesting players. Not much technical information, but an enjoyable read.

Knockout Blackjack – The Easiest Card-Counting System Ever Devised by Olaf Vancura and Ken Fuchs: This book presents the Knock-Out count. It's an unbalanced counting system in which no conversion from running count to true count is required. I respect the system and know many legitimate counters who use it. I still believe the traditional High-Low count to be more powerful but there can be no denying that the Knock-Out is easier to use.

Million Dollar Blackjack by Ken Uston: Although a bit dated, this book is a classic from one of the greatest minds and most interesting characters ever to emerge from the blackjack world. *MDB* contains five levels of strategy from basic to the Uston Advanced Point Count, including the Uston Simple Plus/Minus and Advanced Plus/Minus. There are also plenty of stories from Uston's exciting life as a professional blackjack player.

Playing Blackjack as a Business by Lawrence Revere: At one time, this was probably the best book on blackjack but it has since become dated. Revere has the best treatment of the basic strategy I have ever seen; many of the tables are in color, which makes memorization easier. Revere explains clearly and mathematically his argument that you can make a lot of money playing blackjack.

Professional Blackjack by Stanford Wong: Every book by Wong is truly outstanding, but I consider *Professional Blackjack* his best. Wong introduces the High-Low count and gives complete index numbers for almost every rule variation imaginable, including many unusual rules I've never seen. There are also several appendices of interesting statistics. While it's not for the beginner, it's the gold standard on card counting.

The Theory of Blackjack by Peter A. Griffin: Just as the title says, this book covers the theory of blackjack. The book is very mathematically advanced and presumes a strong background in card counting. This book was not meant to help the typical counter's game but reads more like a college text exploring the math behind card counting. For the person with an academic interest in blackjack you can't sink your teeth much deeper into the game than this.

Turning the Tables on Las Vegas by Ian Andersen: Perhaps the most respected source of information on how not to get barred. There's also a good treatment of the mechanics of card counting.

The World's Greatest Blackjack Book by Lance Humble and Carl Cooper: Although the title is rather pretentious, there can be no serious debate that it's one of the best blackjack books on the market. A great deal of information is packed into its pages. The book covers basic strategy to the Hi-Opt I count strategy.

Pai Gow Poker

Optimal Strategy for Pai Gow Poker by Stanford Wong: As usual for a Stanford Wong book, this one is about as good as it gets for this game. The book explains why the rules in southern California are the best for playing pai gow poker, and presents strategies designed for playing against other good players, as opposed to the casino house way.

Poker

Get the Edge at Low-Limit Texas Hold'em by Bill Burton: This book covers the basics of hold 'em. Targeted to beginners, it is easy to read and has lots of stories and examples from the author's own experience. Unlike other poker books I've read, it doesn't emphasize memorizing hands and the best ways to play them, but rather understanding the reasons behind the plays.

Super System 2 by Doyle Brunson (with several guest contributors): Recently updated, this huge 600+-page book presents strong information written by experts in several different games.

The Theory of Poker by David Sklansky: Many consider this classic to be the most important fundamental poker book available. Lots of math and theory, but grasping the concepts outlined within will set you on the road to becoming a successful poker player.

Sports Betting

Sharp Sports Betting by Stanford Wong: A must-read book for any serious sports bettor. Wong discusses how to improve your odds on everything from straight bets to parlays and teasers. It's rather math heavy, but Wong provides sample problems and solutions. This is certainly one of the most worn out of the many gambling books on my shelf.

Video Poker/Slots

Video Poker Strategy Cards: Take computer-perfect strategies with you when you play the machines. The *Dancer/Daily Strategy Cards* have four levels of strategy (beginner to advanced) for nine different video poker schedules.

Video Poker Software: Learn as you play and use the software to analyze any hand. Currently tops in the field are *Bob Dancer*

Presents WinPoker and *Frugal Video Poker*. Another good software program is *Video Poker Strategy Master* by TomSki, which can produce a strategy table for almost any game (*Frugal Video Poker* has a similar feature).

The Frugal Gambler by Jean Scott: This book is all about milking the casinos for free meals, rooms, and other freebies. It's not hard to have an entire Vegas trip paid for by getting the most out of coupons and slot clubs. Jean Scott shows you how to do it. Nobody knows the topic better than the Queen of Comps.

Million Dollar Video Poker by Bob Dancer: Dancer milked video poker for all it was worth and this is the story of how he did it, turning a bankroll of a few thousand into more than a million. Video poker today is not as lucrative as it was in the '90s, but this is still an informative and enjoyable read.

More Frugal Gambling by Jean Scott and Angela Sparks: This is the follow-up to Scott's *The Frugal Gambler*. Both books contain great advice on how to get the most out of Vegas on a tight budget.

The Slot Expert's Guide to Playing Slots by John Robison: This compact little book provides honest and up-to-date information about the reel slots. No winning strategies (because there are none for the slots), but valuable information for slot players.

Gambling General

Beyond Counting by James Grosjean: Grosjean is a professional gambler whose philosophy is that every game has vulnerabilities that can be exploited and beaten. Chapter by chapter, he goes through games that most consider unbeatable and sheds new light on them. The book is very math heavy, and only appropriate for the top 0.1% of gamblers. It's out of print, but if you're willing to work hard for an edge, try to find a copy any way you can.

Casino Tournament Strategy by Stanford Wong: Playing tournaments can be both fun and profitable. As far as I know, this is the only book devoted solely to maximizing your odds while playing them. The advice covers many games, and the basic principles are applicable in all tournaments.

Comp City – A Guide to Free Casino Vacations by Max Rubin: The best book available on casino comps, which can be as valuable as cash winnings.

Extra Stuff – Gambling Ramblings by Peter Griffin: Several high-level gambling concepts are addressed in this compilation of Griffin's works. Excellent information, but another book best left to the math-oriented.

Finding the Edge by Olaf Vancura, William R. Eadington, and Judy A. Cornelius: This is a collection of academic papers covering a host of gambling topics. Some of the greatest minds in gambling have contributed papers. This book is not for beginners.

Gambling Wizards – Conversations With the World's Greatest Gamblers by Richard W. Munchkin: This book is a collection of interviews with some of the most successful gamblers in the world. It probably isn't what you expect. From golf to backgammon there are plenty of great stories to keep you turning the pages. I read the whole thing in a week, which is very unusual for me.

Gambling Fiction

The Counter by Kevin Blackwood: The story follows the character of Raven as he falls from his Baptist faith and deep into the life of a professional gambler. He starts out as a card counter, but once he wears out his welcome in Las Vegas he takes up with dubious characters in other, more dangerous and illegal, gambling schemes. The author is a former card counter and his depiction of the technical elements of counting and other winning strategies is honest and accurate.

Dice Angel by Brian Rouff: This 222-page novel follows the story of Jimmy, a cynical Las Vegas bar owner, and his efforts to save his bar. After a robbery and embezzlement by his accountant, Jimmy must come up with a lot of money on short notice or lose the bar to the IRS. As a last resort, he turns to the "dice angel," who promises to turn his luck around at craps. Every scene is rich in humor, as Jimmy encounters everything ridiculous about Las Vegas at every turn.

Gambling Other Sources

Newsletter: If you visit Vegas even once a year, you'll want to subscribe to *Anthony Curtis' Las Vegas Advisor.* Lots of updates on Las Vegas gambling conditions, plus gambling coupons for *LVA* members.

Web Sites: Find me on the Web at www.wizardofodds.com. The sister site to the *Las Vegas Advisor* print newsletter is at www.LasVegasAdvisor.com.

Radio: Hosted by Larry Grossman most of the year and Fezzik during the summer, "You Can Bet on It" covers sports betting and other gambling topics on AM radio 1460 in Las Vegas.

Appendix I

Index of Tables

About the Author

Michael Shackleford was born in Pasadena, California, in 1965. He took after his father with an interest in math, and after graduating from the University of California-Santa Barbara, landed a job as an actuary for the Social Security Administration. There he largely analyzed effects of changes in the Social Security laws. In 1997 he compiled his first list of the most popular baby names, to avoid choosing a trendy name for his own child. The baby-name popularity lists took on a life of their own and since then numerous newspapers, magazines, and books have reprinted them.

Also in 1997, he introduced his Web site on gambling, The Wizard of Odds. It began as a non-profit site, but also quickly took on a life of its own. In 2000 he left his job to devote full time to the Web site and a consulting business for the gaming industry.

Today he keeps busy with his Web site, wizardofodds. com, analyzing new casino games for game inventors, designing slot machines, teaching a casino math class at the University of Nevada-Las Vegas, and serving as a consultant to land-based and Internet casinos around the world. In addition to juggling his busy work schedule, he keeps active with two young children, and hiking the mountains around Las Vegas.